major st
PUBLISHING

A CEO's Story from Business Success to Success in Life

ENRICHED
re-defining wealth

John Sikkema

www.enriched.com

First published in 2012 by Major Street Publishing Pty Ltd
© John Sikkema 2012 and 2016

The moral rights of the author have been asserted
National Library of Australia Cataloguing-in-Publication data:

Author: Sikkema, John.
Title: Enriched : re-defining wealth / John Sikkema.
ISBN: 9780987368232 (pbk.)

Subjects: Self-actualization (Psychology)
         Success.
         Conduct of life.

Dewey Number: 158.1

Design: Keston Muijs and Richard O'Gorman
Photography: Jesper Nielsen
Printed in China by Asia Pacific Offset

10 9 8 7 6 5 4 3 2

ISBN 978-0-9873682-3-2

❝ John Sikkema was living the good life, but felt something was missing. In this provocative book, he shares his story and seven life-changing principles that will help you become the person you were created to be. Along the way, you'll also learn how to align the work you do with the person you are, instead of the other way around. Reading *Enriched* could well be a turning point in your life. **❞**

– Ken Blanchard,
Co-author of *The One Minute Manager®* and *Great Leaders Grow*

❝ *Enriched* will prove to be of great value to many people contemplating a deep desire to find more meaning and purpose in their lives, rather than that which the frantic pursuit of money and position has up to now provided them. In a culture which under-values the wisdom and experience of elders, this is a transparently honest, insight-packed and easily-read book that will help many to transform their own lives and positively impact those around them at the same time. **❞**

– Hon John Anderson AO,
Former Deputy Prime Minister of Australia (1999-2005)

❝ In *Enriched*, John Sikkema gives you a powerful strategic plan (blueprint) for undertaking a second-half career that is full of adventure and significance. By the time you get to the last page you will know what you need to do. I could not stop reading this book, I loved it and it hits right where MANY men and women are these days. John's story will change lives! **❞**

– Dean Niewolny,
CEO, Halftime, Dallas, Texas

" It is my hope that *Enriched* will inspire and encourage others to follow in John's footsteps, and that each one of us will reach out and empower others in our sphere of influence to follow his example. I compliment John for his bold initiative in writing this book. It is a new and refreshing perspective that challenges the old paradigms of success and pursuit of wealth and opens our respective world-views to live purpose-driven lives. **"**

– David Bussau AM,
Co-founder of Opportunity International

" Reading this book is like having a conversation with a wise mentor. John Sikkema shares honestly from both his successes and failures to help you turn your career into your passion. *Enriched* will inspire you to do what you've always wanted to do with your life but didn't think was possible. *Enriched* is totally new and fresh (which is hard to believe with millions of books in the world) – it is an honest, from-the-heart account guiding the reader to a new and exciting place in their calling and purpose. **"**

– Markus Koch,
CEO, Daniels International

" *Enriched* is an inspiring read. If we all pick up this responsibility to do a little or a lot within our own capacity to make the world a better place, what a great lift it will give to one's wellbeing and self-esteem. **"**

– Frank Costa OAM,
Chairman of Costa Group; Former Mayor and President
of Geelong Football Club, Melbourne

❝ Life is an adventure and *Enriched* is the best kind of adventure story. It's funny, it's poignant, it's insightful, it's real and it's a great read. What are the factors that make for a great life? What are the attitudes and mindsets that make it possible to not only achieve goals in life but allow you to do so with your integrity intact, your wife still in love with you, your children proud of their Dad, and your own heart satisfied that you have made your years count for something of value? **❞**

– Dr Allan Meyer
CEO Lifekeys

❝ What an incredible book. Successful CEO and entrepreneur, John Sikkema, tells his story – of the hurdles and challenges he faced that brought him to the brink of losing the most significant things/people in his life. In doing so, he redefined wealth. *Enriched* is a must read for all those in leadership roles!" **❞**

– Dr Glenn Williams
CEO, Outward Looking International

❝ At some point in every person's life journey, questions about the meaning and purpose of life emerge. John Sikkema in *Enriched* has navigated this important territory well and is an excellent guide for us. This book is full of wisdom and insight. Highly recommended! **❞**

– Mark Conner
Senior Pastor, CityLife Church, Melbourne

❝ This is a book of hope and optimism. Its message is powerful: the talents that you have been given can help change the world! You've probably helped your company grow, but what if those same talents and skills could be used for a greater good? In *Enriched*, John Sikkema shows how you can turn your career success into a legacy of hope and healing. Do yourself a favour and read it. You won't be able to put it down. **❞**

– Lisa McInnes-Smith
International Speaker Hall of Fame – USA

❝ Do you ever get the feeling that there's something 'better' out there for you? There is! In *Enriched* John Sikkema shares his own remarkable story with brutal honesty and offers practical guidance to help you navigate your own life journey. Conventional wisdom says work hard, save your money and you'll have a great retirement. John tosses in a hand grenade and shows us a new way to live! A must read – if you follow John's advice in this book, your life and others' lives will never be the same. **❞**

– Jossy Chacko
Founder and President of Empart Inc.

❝ A remarkable story! Many similarities to successful Asians who are making a great living, but missing out on life. In *Enriched*, John Sikkema combines stories of both his successes and failures, giving us insight, hope and practical wisdom to move from purely a success focus to one of significance. It will inspire you to review, renew, reconnect, re-ignite and re-invent yourself and to reclaim the life you've always dreamed of living. One that can count for something bigger than yourself! **❞**

– San Wee,
Chairman of Learning Point Group, Singapore

To Sue, my wife. Thank you for teaching me the value and importance of relationships over tasks, and for all your incredible support, patience and love you've shown to me and our four precious children throughout this roller coaster of a life journey. It continues to be an exciting adventure with you!

To Tim O'Neill, my close friend and former business partner. Thank you for helping develop my ideas and dreams into clear vision and strategies whilst sharing my values, passion and convictions to not only build two successful national companies, but importantly beyond that, to impact and change lives.

I will forever be indebted to both of you for encouraging me to live and fulfil my life's purpose.

About the author

John Sikkema's entrepreneurial career began as an eleven year old in Tasmania, Australia, when he spotted a business opportunity literally hiding in the bushes.

At a prestigious golf course near his home, John would seek out wayward golf balls from the surrounding scrub, polish them up, and resell them to unsuspecting players.

By 26, he was earning the same annual salary as the Australian Prime Minister of the day, Malcolm Fraser.

And at 49, as CEO and major shareholder of the financial planning group Garrisons, he sold the business to a Packer backed company for $40 million. He had transformed the small company he started in Tasmania into a successful franchise business with 65 offices across Australia. Yet it was his personal transformation that remains his most satisfying and rewarding achievement.

Today John divides his time between serving on several boards, and his new 'second-half career' as the Executive Chairman of Halftime Australia (www.halftime.org.au), an enterprise devoted to helping others enrich their lives through the discovery of their true purpose.

He lives with his wife, Sue, in Melbourne, Australia. They have four adult children.

Contents

Contents

Foreword by Bob Buford

Since I wrote *Halftime* in 1994, something of a movement has emerged in the United States. Hundreds of thousands of men in their mid-forties and beyond – and an increasing number of women – have discovered that the very best and most fulfilling years of their life are ahead of them. I call it the 'second half'. Unlike our great grandfathers, whose life expectancy was around fifty years, today's forty-year-old can expect another entire lifetime – thirty to forty years – of healthy, productive living. And whereas the generation previous to my own looked forward to retirement, most of us see nothing particularly attractive about terminal leisure.

At the same time, however, we generally have found that pursuing our work solely for the sake of success or increased wealth offers diminishing returns. As many successful people have discovered, growing your net worth may gain you more money, but it doesn't give you a life. And the thrill of the chase that sustained us in our twenties and thirties no longer delivers what we thought it promised. It's not that hard work and contributing to your profession are wrong. It's just that at some point in the first half of your life you begin asking questions:

How much is enough?

Is this what I want to be doing for the rest of my life?

In all that I am gaining, what am I missing?

The inner desire to move from making a living to making a difference is universal in the developed world. It is what opened John Sikkema's heart to a still, small voice that told him he could not go on living as he was, and because he had the courage to listen and make some 'mid-course corrections' in his life, he's well into a productive, adventurous second half.

As am I. In fact, I am now in the third decade of my second half and still have no plans to retire. Instead, I'm still working on things that provide immeasurable significance for me because they relate directly to my life mission. When I took over my family's cable television business, my goal was to make money, and we did. Lots of it. And although I look back fondly at my first-half years, I can honestly say I am having more fun and experiencing more fulfilment in my second half.

And so can you. In *Enriched*, John artfully weaves a tapestry of personal story, practical guidance and inspiring encouragement. He will help you discover what you are most passionate about and how to match that passion with the knowledge, skills and talent you have been given. If you find that appealing – if you want your life to count for something beyond the value of your portfolio or the title on your business card – you have come to the right place.

As a good friend and recovering venture capitalist once said to me, "People have it backwards. Most people worry about what they will sacrifice in the second half. The sacrifice is in the first half – the travel, the stress, the triviality of so much of it. The second half is where the real joy is."

In John's case, he found his life was enriched by investing in others so that they could become more successful. That's where he found "real joy". With his help, you are about to discover your own source of joy.

Bob Buford

Author of *Halftime*, an American Best-seller

Introduction

Immediately after I had completed my role as CEO of our financial planning group, the phone began ringing. "Would you come and speak at our conference?" Or, "We'd love to have you lead a seminar for our organisation."

Word had spread about how I had succeeded in building such a fast-growing and successful national company from Hobart, a provincial city on the island state of Tasmania.

The attendees of these seminars were mostly owners of small businesses. After I had spoken, several would approach me and ask if I would be available to coach them on an ongoing basis. Because so many were located in different cities all over Australia, I had to say no to most of them.

For those who I did help, we often spent a half or whole day in a strategic planning session. I would usually meet with these business owners in their boardrooms and have a great time brainstorming and roughing out a plan to take their business to the next level over the next one to three years. The meetings invariably ended on a high note, as they now saw a constructive way to move forward.

But I would finish with one last question: "Do you have a plan for your own personal life, distinct from your business?" Silence, followed by, "Not really."

Then I discovered a very interesting truth.

As I probed deeper, asking them about their families and aspirations, they would suddenly get very passionate about their personal dreams, which had been put on hold while they pursued the 'business' of building wealth and attaining success. What seemed to really matter to them had been buried in their subconscious or given a low priority because life had become too busy. You could say they were rich on paper, but their lives were not yet enriched by a sense of purpose and meaning.

I myself was nearly a casualty of this type of business and financial success by doing the opposite – that is, trying to somehow make my life-purpose fit my business goals. It seems silly now, but back then it appeared to be a normal path to take.

During those one-on-one business coaching sessions, we often needed to double-back and modify the business plan so that it became more aligned with their personal dreams and aspirations. This was what I had personally and painfully discovered in my own life through a series of events that got my attention. Ultimately, it led me to redefine wealth and make the transition from simply being rich to having an enriched life.

I traced the birth of my second half career out of this simple market research conducted with these men and women who sought my advice. And, ultimately, these conversations provided the motivation to produce something bigger – this book.

Over the last few decades there have been an enormous number of leadership books written, most of which provide ideas, methods, formulas and experiences on how to become more successful in business. I have personally benefited from reading and applying the principles from many of these books in my own life and business. I am forever grateful to these authors, as I would not be where I am today without their books and the ideas they convey. The exceptional ones have been catalysts to help me make important paradigm shifts: *E Myth* by Michael Gerber, *7 Habits of Highly Effective People* by Stephen Covey, *Good to Great* by Jim Collins and *Maverick* by Ricardo Semler. However, the more success I achieved in my business, the more challenges I encountered. Much to my frustration, I could not find the answers to some of these important challenges in the usual business success books.

My aim in writing *Enriched* is to share the answers I discovered to those questions that were unanswered in the success books I had read. I hope this book will also help you experience transformation in your life as I did in mine.

I now devote the majority of my time to encouraging others to discover their life-purpose, and with that clarity help them develop a plan to achieve it. By most standards, these people are already 'successful'. Many are running a thriving business or are in the middle of a remarkable career. But they all have this vague sense that something is missing; life hasn't turned out exactly as they had hoped it would. So I help them refocus and develop a plan to align their business or career to their life-purpose.

The results have been liberating, transformational and truly amazing.

Few things make me happier than seeing someone 'get it', and then make the necessary changes that deliver a life that is far more exciting and fulfilling than the one they had previously. If you are open to some unconventional thinking and have the desire and tenacity to apply the principles I outline in this book, you too can know what it's like to reclaim the life you've always dreamed of living.

John Sikkema,
Melbourne, July 2012

Part 1 The Pursuit of Success

Success – 1. the favourable or prosperous termination
of attempts or endeavours. 2. the gaining of wealth,
position, or the like. 3. a successful performance or
achievement. 4. a thing or a person that is successful.

– Macquarie Dictionary

" WINNING ISN'T EVERYTHING, IT'S THE ONLY THING... "

– Vince Lombardi

1 Is this success?

It was one of those moments when everything in my world was going exactly as I had hoped it would. My wife, Sue, and I were standing in the living room of our new dream home and I could barely contain the sense of accomplishment that welled up inside me. With the help of one of Australia's best architects and a talented team of craftsmen, I had transformed a steep, treed block on Tasmania's South-East coast into our own personal oasis.

It reflected my appreciation for nature and quality. The exterior consisted of second-hand and convict-made bricks that I had handpicked from an old bank in Hobart and a hospital in Launceston. I had chosen these bricks specifically because they blended in with the natural beauty of the picturesque surroundings and spoke quietly of Tasmania's convict history. I also selected large Oregon beams and stained them so that the grain would suggest a ruggedness found in the coastal environment.

EN**RICH**ED

Raised in the church – though not necessarily devout – I added touches to our home that subtly invoked a sense of the sacred. Pyramid-shaped windows into the atrium suggested the Trinity and a cross-shaped skylight bathed the floor in a dazzling pattern of sunlight by day, and by night revealed the luminous splendour of the moon and stars. It almost seemed the Almighty himself was placing his stamp of approval on all I had done.

I had carefully selected this unique property for its privacy and secluded entrance, set high above Kingston Beach; it offered sensational views of the small town where I grew up. In fact, I could stand on the deck and look down on three particular areas that had a profound influence on me during my childhood: the beach, the golf course and the village church where I spent nearly every Sunday.

In a very real sense, this house was my declaration that I had arrived. I had finally made it. The great British Prime Minister, Benjamin Disraeli wrote, "Diligence is the mother of good fortune", and if nothing else, I had put my time in to get to this point in my career. It hadn't been easy. After starting out at the bottom of the ladder, I was well on the way to climbing to the top of my profession, eventually owning my own business, and this house symbolised for me the culmination of a lot of hard work and sacrifice. While I was raised by traditional Dutch parents and had never been overly materialistic, with the creation of this house I shed much of my inherited frugality.

It was stunning. Elegant yet understated. And it was a far cry from the rodent-infested shack I lived in as a child when we first migrated to Australia.

It was proof that I had won first place in the race; evidence of my success.

On this particular occasion, the one where this story began (with me proudly admiring our new home and my wife standing beside me with misty eyes), I had just returned from a rather stressful day at my office. The mere act of pulling into the driveway began to dissipate the tension that goes with running a business. The sun was just dipping into the Derwent River and the bright full moon overhead cast a warm, golden glow over the rustic exterior of our home.

It was enough to bring joy to a man's heart.

With a spring to my step, I jumped out of the car, swung my soft leather briefcase by my side and crossed the small wooden bridge that led to our front door. I remember thinking "life really is pretty good!" I could hardly wait to change into something comfortable, take a cold drink to the deck and let the gentle sea breeze blow away any remnants of the day's hectic agenda. The kids were in bed and after Sue welcomed me home with a quick hug, we just stood there, taking it all in.

That's when it started.

The high price of success

My friend Bob Buford calls it "success panic:" the first whisper of doubt about the value of all you have attained. While I stood there quietly with my wife by my side and surveyed the understated elegance around us, my satisfying sense of accomplishment slowly faded as I considered the true cost of this home, and it had nothing to do with money.

On the surface I really *did* have it made. But strip all that away and what did I really have?

A headache.

Lots of them. Headache pain so debilitating that often when I got home from work I went straight to my bedroom, closed the curtains and lay motionless in the dark. Pain so excruciating I couldn't manage to eat, let alone have dinner with the family. Sue would caution the kids to be extra quiet so as not to disturb their father who was having another one of his migraines.

I tried everything to get rid of them; traditional medicine, non-traditional medicine. Home remedies generously offered to me by friends. The only advice that had a ring of truth to it came from a close friend: "John, you're working too hard. Slow down and I reckon they'll go away."

But I couldn't. The faster my business grew, the more it demanded from me. It wasn't unusual for me to leave the house before anyone else was awake and not return until Sue had already put the younger kids to bed. In order to expand my business to meet the growing demands of the market, I added new employees or acquired other businesses, and that required additional capital. So I had to borrow heavily. Always in the back of my mind a disturbing thought hovered: one slip and the whole business could come tumbling down under the weight of debt.

"Why can't I just enjoy this moment and celebrate my success?" I thought to myself.

As I tried to shift my mind from my business to my lovely family, a troubling wave of guilt engulfed me as I remembered the many soccer games and school activities I had missed.

It didn't seem fair.

Like most men, I thought I was doing the noble thing. I had been a responsible father and husband. I had made sacrifices for my family. I could have settled for a less demanding career and perhaps enjoyed life a bit more, but I put in the long hours and dealt with a stressful job so that I could provide a better life for my family. This house was but one of many 'rewards' they got from all my hard work.

But standing in that serene yet empty living room, I came to the horrific realisation that I hardly knew my children.

Sue's presence next to me should have been comforting, except for the fact that I knew better. To be honest, she was there beside me more out of duty than devotion. The long hours away from home, coupled with my take-charge personality, had taken their toll. And as much as I didn't want to admit it, this was not our dream house, but *mine*.

Who could ask for more?

Only a few years earlier, we had been happily living near the bustling city of Melbourne. We owned a lovely ranch-style home on twenty acres of land and Sue was able to train and ride the young horse she adored. It was a perfect set-up. The children had space to roam around freely and it was only an hour's drive to the city that Sue loved so dearly. She would regularly go there on shopping excursions, exploring the many boutiques and coffee shops, and each year eagerly took the children to visit the Royal Melbourne Show. Melbourne offered her everything she cherished and she would have been more than happy to have spent the rest of her life there. In fact, that was exactly what she thought we would do.

But I wanted to move to Tasmania. After all, it was where I grew up. The kids would finally be close to their grandparents, aunts, uncles and cousins. They could be raised in the same church community where I had been raised. Instead of being a small fish in the big pond of Melbourne, I would be a big fish in a new and growing market in Tasmania. It all made sense.

At least to me.

When I announced that we would be moving to Tasmania, you could see the hurt in Sue's eyes. She had learned from many years of living with me that this wasn't up for discussion, so she tried to put on a brave face. But I could see that the great plan I had just imposed on her crushed her spirit. Perhaps a kinder, gentler husband would have demonstrated some compassion, but at the time, I thought she was just acting like a spoiled child and secretly rationalised that it would be good for her to sacrifice a little. Isn't that what I had done? This would be her turn, and once she saw the house I was planning to build for her, she would change her mind. It didn't help when I also told her she would have to sell her horse.

What began as a joy-filled moment in the living room of my dream house was now just another hollow moment that had become so commonplace in our marriage. The haunting sting of Sue's words on that evening pierced my heart, not so much because she dared utter them but because I knew they were true: "John, you've become boring. You're no fun anymore."

I tried to pull her close, but sensed that stiffness that had crept into our relationship. Generally, I am not an emotional man, but at that moment I felt something well up inside of me that felt like tears. I so wanted to believe that all my hard work, the dream house, living next to family and attending the church near where I had grown up would bring Sue to her senses. I wanted to believe I could engineer our marriage as I had done my career: systematically and with a ruthless drive for success. I thought I had made all the right moves to ensure her happiness. But as I released my grip and she slowly walked away, I couldn't help but recall the words she had said to me a few nights earlier after another exhausting argument: "John, I'm not sure I want to be married to you."

" START BY DOING WHAT'S NECESSARY; THEN DO WHAT'S POSSIBLE; AND SUDDENLY YOU ARE DOING THE IMPOSSIBLE. "

– St Francis of Assisi

24. "START BY DOING WHAT'S
NECESSARY, THEN DO WHAT'S
POSSIBLE, AND SUDDENLY YOU
ARE DOING THE IMPOSSIBLE."

2 The underdog

The downside of my success crept up on me from nowhere. One minute, I was trying to provide for my family, the next I was feeding the ambition inside me that craved acceptance, money, possessions and the feeling of winning against all odds.

How did I get to this point in my life?

It all started back in 1956 when my dad decided to move his family from our comfortable two-storey brick house in Amsterdam, Holland, to what appeared to be a wild frontier outpost on an island off the south coast of Australia. Any further south and you practically fall off the globe.

My father was a well-educated, hard-working family man and during the Second World War he spent many years in the merchant navy with regular periods of onshore leave in the USA. He loved the positive business environment that existed there, so when he saw that Australia offered similar opportunities and that his two brothers and sister had also moved 'Down Under', the decision to migrate from Europe was quickly made.

My mother wasn't so fond of the idea. First of all, she didn't speak a word of English and she had three young children, including me, my older sister Nell and our baby brother Jack to care for. Luckily, at age five, you don't see things the way adults do. While it seemed the further we got from Europe the more my mother cried, for me it was all an exciting adventure. Five weeks crossing oceans on board a ship. The discovery by ship authorities that a criminal was on board and the drama of seeing him apprehended and locked up. Cruising through the Suez Canal as leather-faced traders nudged up alongside in barges to barter handbags and souvenirs to passengers on deck. The bumpy aeroplane ride – my first – in an old propeller-driven Fokker Friendship from Melbourne to Hobart. As far as I was concerned, I was living a charmed life.

Fitting in

Once we landed on solid ground, reality sunk in.

Seeing my mother cry at the sight of our first house in Australia really underscored for me just how much I didn't fit into my new surroundings. That old lopsided weatherboard shack at the end of a dead-end road in Blackman's Bay, with its sloping floor and a healthy population of mice inside – and the occasional wild pig outside – might as well have been a giant sign reading: 'You're not in Holland anymore!'

But it wasn't until my first day of school that I truly understood the meaning of being a foreigner.

Imagine sitting at your desk in an unfamiliar schoolroom surrounded by people who speak a strange-sounding language that you do not understand. The teacher says something and everyone opens their books to a certain page – everyone but you, because you couldn't understand the teacher's directions. Immediately, one of the students stands and apparently reads from the book, then sits down as the teacher smiles and speaks again in that gibberish that makes no sense to you at all. Then another student stands and does the same thing, and with horror you realise it will soon be your turn to stand and read. But you not only don't know what page everyone else is on; the words on *every* page might as well be in Chinese characters.

EN**RICH**ED

For the first time in my life, my Dutch heritage loomed as a giant liability standing in the way of the one thing I wanted: acceptance.

I was a foreigner. I spoke the wrong language. I even *looked* different (something not helped by the girlish-looking jumpers I wore that my mum knitted for me). I'm not proud of it, but right then and there I decided to become like everyone else. I not only taught myself English, but shocked and disappointed my mother by refusing to speak Dutch at home. As for the hand-made clothes, I added insult to injury to my mother by either 'losing' them or refusing to wear them. Our meagre family income was allocated into a series of glass expense jars that lined a wooden shelf – a primitive yet effective form of budgeting. There was no jar labelled 'proper Australian clothing', yet somehow my mother found some extra pennies for clothes for me.

Trying to shed my Dutch culture, however, wasn't enough. I didn't just want to be accepted, I wanted to be respected. I quickly discovered that in Australia, sport is practically a religion. So, when the 'new kid' started beating everyone in playground races, his status rose quickly. I could run fast – really fast. So fast that I was selected to represent my school at the Anzac Day School Sports Carnival to compete against runners from all the other schools in our district.

This was heady stuff. My event was the 75-yard dash, and after winning several qualifying heats I found myself in the final. Just to have been selected to represent my school was enough to erase all the baggage that came with being a foreigner, but I wanted to win – to take home the champion's trophy for my event. Anything less would have been failure.

Slightly-built compared with the other runners in the final, I nonetheless jogged confidently up to the starting line to await the crack of the starter's pistol. Ten yards down the track, I was ahead of the pack. I had always had a fast start but knew my bigger competitors usually came on strong at the end. Nothing would be worse than getting beaten right at the finish, but I could hear them getting closer as my lungs screamed for more oxygen. I wanted to win. Had to win. Somehow, I just put my head down and ran as hard as I could until I hit the finish line. First place! Finally, I had arrived.

Almost.

Learning the value of hard work

It's one thing to gain the respect of your mates, but I was still painfully aware that I didn't have a lot of the things they had. There just wasn't enough money in those jars my parents kept on the shelf at home to pay for them. Whether I was really poor or just the victim of Dutch frugality, it didn't matter.

I realised that if I was really going to make it in Australia, I would have to take matters into my own small hands.

So began my business career.

Our home was right next to the prestigious private Kingston Beach Golf Club and the majority of the members were part of Hobart's establishment. I began caddying for a barrister from Hobart who paid me seven shillings (when the going rate was five) to carry his heavy bag around the course every Saturday. Along the way I developed a talent for spotting wayward golf balls, which I would sell to the golf professional, who then sold them back to the golfers. It didn't take me long to question the value of a 'middleman'. Instead of caddying each Saturday I decided to set a quota for myself – twenty golf balls – and then see if I could sell directly to the golfers.

Sure enough, I found the twenty balls, raced home and washed them bright and clean in soapy water, then returned to the course and waited under a bridge for a player to walk by. Despite being painfully shy, I somehow mumbled my sales pitch to an unsuspecting golfer and he bought the entire lot!

I raced home with one pound in my pocket – nearly three times what I would have got by simply caddying and double the amount I would have received by selling to the golf pro – and a new appreciation for a sales technique that would later come in handy: the cold call.

Keeping a promise

I couldn't have known it at the time, but having to earn my way in this strange new country developed qualities in my character that would serve me well – and in some cases too well – later in life. For example, one time on the golf course I saw an elderly man, maybe seventy years old or so, drive his ball across the river and into some thick shrubs. I went to help him find it and after about five minutes of stomping around in the long grass saw it peeking out from under some bushes. The old man was so grateful he offered to pay me a shilling for my good deed, but as he rummaged around in his pockets he came up empty. Embarrassed that he didn't have the money he'd promised, he took out a pad of paper and a pencil and asked for my name and address. I tried to refuse but he insisted.

I forgot the incident until about a week later when I received an official-looking envelope in the mail bearing the Governor's wax seal and containing a letter from Lord Rowallan, the Governor of Tasmania – and a shilling!

I was more impressed with the letter than the shilling, because a man of such importance had taken the time to personally write a note of thanks and follow up on his promise to pay me. It made me feel important.

What better way to learn the value of keeping your word as well as the power of affirming others?

By the time I was twelve years old, my golf ball business was thriving, filling my savings jar with enough cash to buy things I had always wanted but my parents couldn't afford – my first bike (second-hand), new clothes, an impressive Swiss watch, and especially lunches from the school canteen as I loathed the soggy homemade tomato sandwiches my mother packed for me. I not only began to see how money helps you get ahead in life, but I learned that I could make money with a simple recipe of enthusiasm, energy and resourcefulness. One year I even bought my own schoolbooks because our family was struggling financially.

Seeing yet another opportunity, on my new bike I began delivering *The Mercury*, Hobart's daily newspaper, climbing out of bed at 5:30 every morning to increase my income by one pound a week. And if I still needed more cash, I always found a way to earn it, by picking cherries during school holidays or taking an occasional Saturday night paper run.

I got it from my mum

After the initial shock of moving to Australia had worn off, my mum Tina's normal positive can-do approach returned with a passion and she soon discovered her own business acumen. She had always been a very strong-willed and determined woman – even from a young age. At just eighteen years old this was apparent when she rode her bicycle ten kilometres through Nazi-occupied Holland straight to the Nazi headquarters. Her elder brother, Menze, had been captured the day before for having ammunition hidden in their house and my mother was determined to get him back. While most offenders were commonly shot and never seen again, after my mother's brave request and skills in persuasion, they set her brother free. It was a miracle. My widowed grandmother was overjoyed with his release and the family business was able to keep running. It's no surprise then that many years later, once she had overcome the initial challenges of migrating to Australia, those same qualities of persuasion came in useful when my mother found a need for them.

Tasmania wasn't like Holland. It was primitive – it was still being settled! The locals lived simply and went without many of the finer things my mother was accustomed to from her life in Europe. She was appalled by the lack of good quality stores and bad customer service and made up her mind to capitalise on the situation.

Against my father's wishes she got a job picking apples and then used the money to buy clothing from wholesalers to resell to farmers. She even convinced my father to teach her how to drive and let her use his aqua-coloured 1965 Ford Falcon with bench seats to sell clothes door-to-door in the country. This was back in the late '60s when women of her age were not often seen driving cars and were expected to stop work once they married. Needless to say, in those days it was a rarity for a woman to start and run her own business.

Watching her little business outgrow our house, and then a small shop she rented, I was fascinated by her success. Eventually, she hired my brother, my sister and even my reluctant father, who left the police force to join her venture. This subservient Dutch wife, who taught herself English, was able to buy two brand new imported Saabs, build an architect-designed house and beach house and pay cash for a holiday unit by the beach on the Gold Coast, Australia's top holiday spot. Not bad for a woman who began by selling clothes out of the back of a car.

Seeing my mum's success and enjoying a bit of my own convinced me that I had the right stuff to make it myself. Although I did okay in high school and matriculation college, I found formal study slow-paced and mostly irrelevant. So instead of going to university, I got a job fresh out of school working in a bank. My Dutch work ethic and problem-solving skills brought more responsibility than a bank would normally give to a kid who was barely shaving, however I quickly discovered that salary was commensurate with age – I wouldn't make full salary until I reached thirty-three years old, regardless of how well I performed!

So what would you do if you were young and adventurous and had already learned you had a knack for making money?

I quit my bank job, drove my sporty little Isuzu Bellette onto the ferry to Melbourne, and then with my friend Donovan drove to Sydney – the financial capital of Australia – to try my luck in the big city.

" THE LADDER OF SUCCESS IS BEST CLIMBED BY STEPPING ON THE RUNGS OF OPPORTUNITY. "

– Ayn Rand

3 Climbing the success ladder

It was 1970 and the year that being called up to serve in the Vietnam War was a real fear. If my birthday was unlucky enough to come up, I would have had to put my move and business ambitions on hold while I served in the army for two years of National Service. Thankfully, my number didn't come up and I was free to pursue success and new horizons.

As a consequence, at age twenty I moved to Sydney where I immediately enrolled in the School of Hard Knocks and soon became one of its stellar students. The first 'knock' against me was the fact I was from Tasmania. It may seem incredulous today, but in the 1970s, people from the mainland were wary of employing Tasmanians as invariably they would move back to their island home. It was a hard stigma to break and for the first time in my life I couldn't find work, even though there were many openings and I applied for most of them. I wasn't too worried, though. I was young, Bondi Beach was a short walk from my apartment, and I bought a brand new surfboard. Nothing wrong with having a little fun before jumping into my 'career.'

After several weeks of trying, I finally landed a job on the assembly line at the British Leyland plant where I sanded car bodies of the Morris 1100 before they were spray-painted. The work was boring and soul-destroying so at lunchtime on my first day I walked out the gate without telling anyone. I must give credit though to British Leyland – a few months later I received a pay cheque in the mail for my half-day's labour!

From there, I signed on at an air-conditioner plant and again was stuck on an assembly line – this time with a team of immigrants who couldn't speak English. I thought I was doing a pretty good job – until they fired me. I was told it was not because of poor performance but because Donovan and I had kept to ourselves as the only two 'Aussies' on site. Apparently, we had failed to mix with the ethnic workers who did not speak English. I sort of saw the irony of this, being the immigrant who could not speak English back at school! It was the first and only time I've ever been fired.

Next, I found myself on the end of a monster-drilling machine at Sydney's Mascot Airport. My job was to drill holes in huge boulders so that a crane could lift them and drop them into the bay, reclaiming land for the airport's expansion. Whilst highly paid, it was back breaking with twelve-hour shifts that were repetitive and dangerous – one of my fellow construction workers was killed when a heavy chain dropped onto him from the crane.

When I learned of an opportunity to go apricot-picking in Wagga Wagga, I jumped at the chance. Compared to wrestling a drill in the blazing Sydney sun, being out in the country in a shady orchard seemed almost too good to be true. It was. When I got there I discovered it was a bit of a scam as most of the fruit had already been picked.

Joining forces

I can't say I was ready to give up on my dream to make it on my own, but all that free time in the orchard only made me miss my Tasmanian girlfriend, Sue, all the more. We had dated regularly prior to me heading off on my mainland adventure, and my thoughts seemed to continually return to her.

We had met at the local town hall the previous year, dancing free-spiritedly to the tunes of The Mixtures – *Pushbike Song* and *In The Summer Time*. Normally, I was quite introverted, but on this particular night when my eyes landed on Sue, I felt a sudden attraction to her unlike any girl I had met.

EN**RICH**ED

First of all she wasn't Dutch, and her surname was easy to pronounce. She was tall and slender with long, dark wavy hair, bright blue eyes and a beautiful smile. Not only was she the prettiest girl at the dance, she was intelligent and had the unique ability to make me feel completely comfortable.

After that night at the dance we started dating and quickly fell in love. But I had already made plans to travel. We shared a spirit of adventure and after moving to Sydney, I came to realise that I wanted to be with her so that this big adventure would not just be mine, but ours. I wanted it to be a dream that we could pursue together.

Since I wasn't exactly racing up the ladder of success, I temporarily halted my adventure and bid a hasty retreat to Tassie. Within a few months Sue and I married and left Tasmania behind together.

In the early days of our marriage, we travelled north to the sunny city of Brisbane and lived a carefree existence in a flat which was part of an old Queenslander house on stilts. It was a beautiful time. We were happy; my blonde hair was down to my shoulders and we did our best to live on love and odd jobs. Every earthly possession we owned fitted on the roof rack of our little car and I suppose we'd still be roaming the country like hippies had we not welcomed a new guest into our lives. Our first child, Alice, was born and with her came a big wake-up call for me.

Maybe I'm just rationalising my relentless drive for success, but when Alice came into our world, it hit me with a mixture of fear and obligation. It wasn't just the fact that we now had an extra mouth to feed, but a real live human being to nurture and protect. I can't say that I made a conscious decision to settle down and try to provide more stability for my little family, but our 'happy wanderer' lifestyle began to seem irresponsible.

The transformation from carefree adventurer to doting father surprised me as much as it did Sue. I couldn't wait to rush home from work to play with Alice and must have kept Kodak in business that year with all the pictures I took of her. Many weekends we would pack a picnic lunch and head off south to the Gold Coast or north to the Sunshine Coast beaches of Queensland.

After knocking around on a few more jobs requiring more brawn than brain – including one where I was working all day on a jackhammer and got my lights punched out by a fellow worker – I entered the world of corporate sales almost by accident.

In the search for work, we travelled from Brisbane to Melbourne and at age twenty-three I found myself repossessing cars for a finance company. While I loved the 'detective' nature of the job, confronting the delinquent owners was a little dicey. What do you say to the European guy who threatens, "You taka my car, I keel you!"

Once, as I was trying to track down the owner of a Chrysler Valiant, I showed up at the office of the T & G Insurance company where he worked and spoke to his boss.

"You're obviously pretty good at what you do," the manager replied after I told him why I was there. "Why don't you come and work for us?"

I told him I'd give it some thought. However, Sue was working as a legal secretary next to the offices of National Mutual Insurance (now AXA) and when she told the National Mutual manager about my unusual job offer, he called me with a better offer – one that I couldn't refuse.

Dressed for success

Finally, I had a job in an office – albeit a bedroom in our two-bedroom flat. Unfazed by the fact that I had no clients, I went out and bought a suit and a brand new orange Datsun 180B. Since I'd learnt to overcome the fear of 'cold calling' from my golf-ball selling days, I was confident I would soon be visiting potential clients and wanted to show up looking like a successful businessman.

My sales plan was simple. Each morning I sat down at my makeshift desk with the Melbourne phone book. Reasoning that my competitors started at the front of the phone book, I turned to the back of the thick directory and began with the Ws. My first day on the job I dialled sixty people whose names began with W. It took me about five hours and yielded only two appointments, but that was fine with me. Just as I had done when I started my golf-ball business, I set a goal: eight appointments a week. Usually, I was able to convert two of these into sizeable sales. I also quickly developed a technique that almost guaranteed the sale of two policies for each prospect. Here's how it worked.

Because I called during the day, housewives usually answered the phone, and I quickly got their attention by offering to set up a savings plan for their children's education. What mum could resist that? I suggested that I could stop by one evening when their husbands were home to explain how the plan would benefit them. Once I gained their trust and sold this policy I was able to set up another appointment to talk with them about life insurance and superannuation. It almost always generated another sale. I even developed a little trick based on the rumpled detective of the 1970s' television program, *Columbo*. After making the sale I would thank them, grab my coat, and head for the front door before turning 'spontaneously' and saying, "Oh before I go, I almost forgot to ask you about your insurance, Mr Jones. I presume you have some and that it's been recently reviewed?" Invariably this opened the way for me to review their family cover and increase it by selling them another policy.

It might not have been the most sophisticated sales strategy, but it worked. After just four months my manager announced at our company's quarterly sales meeting that I was the second highest earning salesman in our region!

Hard work pays off

That first taste of success developed an appetite for more, and I began devising other strategies to get people to buy insurance from me. I was particularly successful in targeting younger people with disposable incomes. I researched the various insurance policies that our company offered and tailored them to suit specific groups of people. I marketed and packaged them in such a way as to make people feel that the policy was designed especially for them.

With success, of course, came money – a lot of it. I remember in 1977 proudly showing my father, who had been sceptical about my choice of a career in insurance, my earnings for that year: $43,000 – the same as Prime Minister Malcolm Fraser (the average annual income then was $5,000).

So you can imagine the surprised looks I got when I announced my resignation, particularly since at the time I was the top salesman out of the three-hundred-strong sales force for National Mutual Victoria.

But by now I was well and truly ready to strike out on my own as this way I could better control my own destiny. Two things motivated me.

Firstly, I wanted to be able to give my clients the best products from all the insurance providers, not just from the one company I happened to work for. By having more and better policies to offer, my clients got a better deal. Even though initially my income dropped as these policies paid lower upfront commissions, I took satisfaction in knowing I was giving them the sort of policy I would buy myself.

Secondly, I was able to achieve my dream of building my own business rather than working for an insurance company. As a broker an added bonus I received was an ongoing trail commission for the life of the policies. Over time, this would ensure I was adequately compensated for being paid the lower amount upfront. Importantly, it meant I was building a saleable asset.

By this time, however, Sue had quit her job and now our little baby Alice had two siblings: Heath and Renee. And there was that mortgage on the twenty-acre property that I had bought to house our growing family.

It wasn't a good time to take on the risks of running my own business, but then again, there never is a good time to start your own business. But for me it was the natural progression.

Australian statistics show that in 2011 one in three businesses failed within the first three years of operation. Back in 1979 it was much the same. But like many entrepreneurs, I was prepared to back myself. You may well recognise this type of confidence and self-assurance from your own new business ventures. Often people may have warned you of the risks involved. They may have said you were crazy to take such a big risk – and yet you still did it.

Leo. F. Buscaglia, best-selling author, motivational speaker and professor at the University of Southern California once famously said, "the person who risks nothing, does nothing, has nothing, and becomes nothing. He may avoid suffering and sorrow, but he simply cannot learn and feel and change and grow and love and live."

I seemed to thrive on risk, and having Sue by my side was an added bonus. We genuinely enjoyed each other's company and shared many similar aspirations.

The immigrant boy from Tassie was finally starting to fit in with the big boys of Melbourne.

" THE ABILITY TO MANAGE WELL DOESN'T MAKE MUCH DIFFERENCE IF YOU'RE NOT EVEN IN THE RIGHT JUNGLE. "

– Stephen R. Covey

4 Back to my roots

For the first time since I sold golf balls, I was once again a business owner with the freedom to develop my own business. It felt fantastic! It was almost like the good old days in our little apartment. I bought a second-hand electric typewriter and Sue composed and then typed up regular batches of my pre-approach letters, which became a great source of new business. In my first year in business on my own, I made a six-figure income – which was well above the average wage back then!

You would think once I finally owned my own modest business and saw my bank account grow, I could relax a little and enjoy life. But deep down, I was still that little Dutch boy trying to prove my worth by winning all the races at the Anzac Day sports carnival. I wanted a much bigger business before I could say I was really successful. I was still very much the underdog trying to prove myself.

Valuing my heritage

At a business level, I might have been succeeding, but cracks were beginning to appear in other areas of my life. At home, things weren't so good. My headaches got worse. There were additional family responsibilities with three young children and I felt the tension of Sue and I increasingly living in two different worlds.

For some time I had found myself missing Tasmania. I worried that our kids didn't really know their extended family; grandparents, cousins, uncles and aunties. The Bass Strait between Melbourne and Tasmania may as well have been the Pacific Ocean.

I was also concerned that my children were being secularised by not living in a Christian community. I had such a rich family heritage in Tasmania – the type of heritage that many people would love to tap into.

Yet I was taking that for granted and denying my children the benefits of their extended family, all for the sake of my business career, our freedom and independence, and the excitement of living near a big city.

Ironically, it was 'excitement' that led us to make an important decision.

Feeling of isolation

One cold winter's night, after working a hectic long day in the city, I arrived home late. We had just gone to bed when the quiet was interrupted by the sound of a car tearing up the long, gravel drive of our property. Headlights flashed up at the house as heavy, loud music erupted into the night. Then, without warning, a sudden crack of gunfire sounded.

"What the heck..." I heard myself yell, as I jumped up.

Peering out from behind the curtains, Sue and I stood side-by-side and watched in horror as a car full of young men came to a halt right outside the house. In my tiredness, I hadn't shut the gate that evening.

"Sue, call the police," I said, trying to stay calm.

Quickly I checked to make sure the house was securely locked as Sue explained to the police, the danger that was unfolding. "Please hurry," she added desperately and hung up the phone.

We could hear the drunken voices of men swearing. Our Border Collie was barking furiously and I feared he may get shot. Incredibly, the car turned around and drove along a side-driveway, which led to a derelict old weatherboard shack, just three hundred metres away.

EN**RICH**ED

I had an idea but it would have to be done quickly. All I had to do was sneak down and reach the metal gate at the end of our driveway. There was a padlock on the gate and it might just be enough to deter the wannabe criminals from venturing any closer to our house, and thus lead them down the main road.

It was a long shot, but worth the risk.

I walked quickly through the trees that lined our driveway. I could still hear the racket from the men close by. As I tiptoed through the grass, Sue's horse walked alongside me and ingeniously provided complete cover as I trailed the fence-line. Finally, I reached the gate, closed it and secured the padlock.

So far so good, I hadn't heard any more gunshots and, hopefully, the police were on their way by now.

As I crept back towards Sue and the house, I could hear the car skidding on the gravel at the end of our driveway, ready to return the way it came, but then it braked outside our locked gate. I heard a tirade of angry, drunken voices yelling at each other, all seemingly confused as to where they were. Then thankfully, they did a u-turn and the car grinded down to the main road, bypassing our house altogether.

Sue opened the front door and quickly let me in and we looked at each other with relief. It was only at that moment that the bright blue and red flashing lights from the police car could be seen, racing through the shadows of the trees. We were safe!

Amid all the panic and mayhem, I suddenly had clarity. My family was vulnerable.

There was no one besides me looking out for them. Thankfully, no one was hurt that night. But the threat to their safety was enough to make me think hard about my family's future. My previous thoughts of moving back to my family and the community I grew up in came flooding back to me.

Sure, it would be challenging if we moved. I would have to start my business from scratch again, I would most likely initially suffer financially.

But I was confident the new skills I had acquired in the big competitive city of Melbourne would put me one step ahead of the game in the much smaller city of Hobart. I figured this would only be a small hiccup. My plan was to have the best of both worlds.

Since I was now my own boss, I made an executive decision. I would take my family back to my roots.

With Sue's reluctant agreement, we moved back to Tasmania and into a big, clumsy rental house in Kingston, about twelve kilometres south of Hobart. Funnily enough, it reminded me of the shack I first migrated to, especially when Sue caught three mice in one day.

But I didn't care – I couldn't look past the positive influence that the move would have on my family, especially my kids.

But one good decision does not mean everything will be easy sailing.

My new partner – Clark Kent

Upon our return to the state of Tasmania – the so-called "Apple Isle", Sue and the kids were quickly embraced by my Dutch family and the church community, just as I had hoped. It was as if we had never left. Our parents loved having their grandchildren and us so close by and I was finally able to focus on my business.

In addition to insurance and superannuation, I added tax planning and investment services to my bow and called my company *Statewide Financial Services*. Once again, my business thrived. Over the next few years, I hired the best talent I could find, merged with another business, and established regional offices in Hobart, Launceston and Burnie – the three main regions in Tasmania.

My best-ever recruit was Tim O'Neill, a young accountant with a confident and enterprising flair who took over the Launceston financial planning side of my business.

Tim wasn't your typical accountant type. From years of following his passions of windsurfing and bush walking, Tim was sun-tanned and fit and when he wore his suit and dark-rimmed glasses he could have easily been mistaken for the clean-cut Clark Kent!

Tim and I had complementary strengths and a chemistry that enabled us to work well together to build the business. With Tim's help, we drafted our first business plan, which stated our vision: "To become the premier financial planning company in Tasmania." At the time, we were the fourth largest, but I relished another 'race'.

Within two years of Tim joining the company, he had become the business partner I had been looking for. I negotiated buying out the other two shareholders and I was now firmly planted in the CEO's chair with a team of twenty-two staff members looking to me expectantly for inspiration and leadership.

Things were going well.

I now had the largest shareholding in the company which we renamed Garrisons and between us Tim and I owned the majority of the shares. I also decided to offer a small amount of the company shares to several of our top planners and key people in our management team to ensure they stayed on board for the ride and would share in the company's success. Yet, while good things were happening, storm clouds appeared on the horizon.

I recently became aware of a book with an intriguing title: *Treat Me Like Your Customer*. The author, Louis Upkins JR, took the title from a comment made by the wife of a very successful businessman in America. I believe the full quote was something like, "I don't expect you to shower me with flowers and kindness, but I just wish you would treat me the same way you treat your customers."

Those words could easily have been spoken by Sue (or my kids, for that matter). While they were enjoying the benefits and support of living in the tight-knit Dutch community of Kingston, the demands of my growing business were taking their toll. There never seemed to be enough time to do everything, and working eighty to ninety hour weeks became the norm. Even when I finally got home, I spent my free time reading business journals, writing reports, or nutting out strategies to solve problems.

Early warning signs

I was smart enough to know you can't go on like that forever, but couldn't seem to find the exit ramp from my frenetic lifestyle. My wife needed me, my children needed me, my business needed me and my staff needed me. Frustration fuelled my headaches and most weeks the pain was so intense I was forced to go home and lie in a quiet room, taking increasing amounts of pain-killers.

Generally not given to self-pity, I confess that many times as I lay motionless in that dark room, life for me didn't seem fair.

Couldn't my children see that all of my hard work gave them their dream house, their designer clothes, their private-school education, and a lot of other nice things I never had when I was their age? Couldn't Sue be more supportive instead of retreating into herself, silently letting me know there was little connecting us anymore?

It seemed that no matter how hard I tried or how many hours I worked, I couldn't achieve the success that I wanted in the sleepier and smaller Tasmanian business marketplace. I felt stretched to the limit emotionally, spiritually, physically, relationally and financially. Much later in life, after my son, Heath, had set out on his own, I asked him about those years when he and his siblings were younger, and his honesty still haunts me: "You were always stressed and exhausted – usually with a headache, and it didn't make you a very fun person to be around. I also remember how you and mum regularly had those high-intensity arguments. I know it was largely due to the pressures of life and the stresses of your business. I used to wonder why my dad couldn't get a regular job on a salary like my friends' dads."

Ouch!

But he was right. And even though I tried to convince myself I was running on empty in order to provide for them, the truth was that I gave too high a priority to my business and as a consequence I neglected my family. I didn't know it at the time. I thought I was doing all the right things a man was supposed to do.

For our entire married life together, I had been in control. I had called all the shots and carefully executed the 'business plan' at work and at home. And on the surface at least, they all seemed to work.

Well, that's what I told myself, even as I inwardly knew that for all my work, I had little to show for it. Success was proving to be a shallow reward for all that it took to achieve, but I didn't know any other way to live.

For the first time in my life, I wasn't so sure I could win this race.

Everything I had worked for, everything I cared about – would it even be here tomorrow?

It was a chilling thought.

Over the years, I had seen other CEOs in my position go under and lose everything they loved; their business, their marriage, the respect of their children, even their health – but I never thought I would be lumped into that awful basket.

I did not like what I had become and neither did Sue.

" **SUCCESS IS A LOUSY TEACHER. IT SEDUCES SMART PEOPLE INTO THINKING THEY CAN'T LOSE. "**

– Bill Gates

5 Wake-up call

Sue and I sat meekly in the marriage counsellor's office. It was my lunch break and I had cancelled an important meeting but I still had to rush to make the one o'clock appointment.

"You're late," Sue whispered crossly as I smiled apologetically and took a seat. Sue had dressed up for the occasion, she looked good and somewhat smug – I suspect because she finally had me cornered and I was not in control – the counsellor was.

After studying me with mild disinterest, the very casually dressed man whose name I had quickly forgotten asked me a question:

"John, how would you rate yourself as a marriage partner? One being poor and ten being excellent?"

EN**RICH**ED

Mulling over my answer, I quickly eliminated ten and reasoned that nine and even eight also seemed too high, given the circumstances I found myself in.

"Six?" I suggested humbly.

I really wanted to say seven.

The marriage counsellor scribbled something down on his pad of paper and nodded impassively.

Next, he asked Sue to score me as a partner. She kept her eyes downwards and quietly gave her number.

"Three. As a marriage partner John is a three out of ten."

I tried to keep my face neutral as I heard the dismal figure. Three? I was not used to failure. Surely not being home to change a light bulb, mow the lawn and missing a few children's teacher interviews didn't equate to such a low score? After all, look at what I brought to the relationship: a nice house, kids in private school, I even regularly took the family on holidays and weekends away – what more did this woman want from me?

Deep down inside, of course, I knew she was right. I wasn't the free-spirited romantic she had married, but I didn't want to admit it. Besides, it's not as if I woke up one day and decided, "I'm going to do my best to be the most irritable, unexciting husband in the world." Life exacts a heavy price from all of us, and for me the cost of success was beginning to feel exorbitant.

More than once Sue had made it clear to me that she could live with a lot less if it would give us a better relationship. I suppose those sentiments were intended to temper my competitive, driven nature but instead they frustrated me all the more. Didn't she realise that as a business leader I needed to portray a successful image? Sure, I could buy a cheaper vehicle and move into a less expensive house, but what would that say about me – especially in such a tight-knit business community as Tasmania?

The truth is, I really didn't care all that much about my image. I loved the chase; thrived on the rush I got from growing my business. Yes, it was nice to make a lot of money and buy nice things, but I wasn't pushing myself so hard just to buy another suit or a fancy toy. For me money was the yardstick I used to measure my success. It validated me; convinced me that I was no longer the underdog immigrant but a rising star in the financial services industry.

More cracks appear

When it came to my personal relationships though, the yardstick to measure success was harder to gauge. It wasn't until we experienced an incident with our daughter Renee that the penny dropped: my parenting skills were way below par.

Of my four children, Renee was by far the most independent. She was a middle child and had more street smarts than the rest of my children put together. If you gave Renee one dollar, she'd quickly make it into two – so you can imagine how living under my roof cramped her style.

One day my youngest daughter, Jessica, came running downstairs with a horrified look on her face.

"Renee's run away from home," she blurted out in a flurry of tears as she handed me a note she found under her sister's pillow.

"I can't live with you anymore... you need to change..."

I winced as I read her messy, scrawled writing. There was no use denying the cause of Renee's hurt – the blame lay squarely with me. My beautiful, teenage daughter was wandering out in the streets or sleeping under a bridge somewhere and it was my fault. I tried to remain calm for

Sue's sake but couldn't shake the potentially awful news headlines from my mind – anything could happen to her out there; she may have been tough but she was small and slim and no match for a full grown man.

Thankfully, after three days of searching, she was found but it wasn't until we sat down face to face that I had to own up to the fact that I had been failing in the most important job of all – being a father. It was one of the worst moments of my life but I didn't know how to change. My daughter needed a dad who could spend quality time with her, someone to give encouragement and understanding through her changing teenage years. This 'job description' was so far removed from my role as CEO in the workplace that I couldn't seem to make the switch.

I was the boss at work and I was boss at home. The only difference was at the office my employees were paid to be there and could leave at any stage. At home, my children had no choice. I was it. And unfortunately for them, too often I was so stressed out from running a business, my tank was completely empty and there was nothing left to give.

Addiction to work

Working hard isn't in itself a bad thing. But on the road to success, I had developed an addiction and it was affecting everyone around me – especially my kids.

I was a workaholic. "Who isn't?" I can hear you thinking. With more pressure to work long hours, skip lunch breaks and take shorter holidays, it's a wonder that there are any healthy, well-balanced workers still left.

Some experts view it as a serious psychiatric disorder, much like alcoholism or a drug addiction – yet it's the only one society rewards.

"You were the first one in the office and the last to leave and you worked through your entire weekend? You are the type of employee who will go places!"

"You came in early, rather than exercising and wasting time. That is so appreciated you are next in line for a promotion…"

According to a recent survey, thirty-four per cent of adults don't take their holidays – many citing work obligations as the reason they couldn't leave the office. Others admitted that even when they did take time off, it was hard to relax and enjoy that time – they were too stressed out.

I'm ashamed to admit it, but on nearly every single one of my "holidays" with the family I spent the majority of the time on the phone fixing emergencies back at the office or lying on the couch with a migraine. I also had the habit of cutting short every vacation. It was so commonplace, the kids actually anticipated after five days away they might have to pack their bags at any given time. Hardly a relaxing break away.

It will not come as any surprise then that this same survey found the divorce rate of couples where one partner was a workaholic was almost three times higher than in 'normal' couples. I commonly hear of couples who both work on their laptops in bed until the late hours of the night, both still frantically working; they may have left the office, but things are far from over.

The problem is when you are in your "business bubble" which consumes most of your waking hours, it's hard to do anything other than fight on and that's what I did.

And thanks to an American President, I couldn't stop and try to figure it all out. I will reserve judgment on President George H. W. Bush's decision to go to war with oil-rich Iraq, other than to say it wasn't the best thing for my business. Not that he cared, but I did. Today, $50 for a barrel of oil sounds like a bargain, but in 1991 it was a huge jump causing a wave of inflation that, according to Australia's

Prime Minister at the time, Paul Keating, could only be stopped with "the recession we have to have." Then the Reserve Bank of Australia lifted the interest rates pushing some home mortgages as high as seventeen per cent! Hordes of borrowers lost their homes and many small businesses closed up shop.

Business under threat

Not a great time to be in the financial services business. Few people had money to invest – most were looking to cash in whatever investments they had. In those days we received virtually no commission on cash or fixed-interest investments.

Our business was haemorrhaging $30,000 to $40,000 a month and in no time had amassed debts of about $700,000, for which Tim and I personally were liable. We considered the obvious option that many companies take when their backs are up against the wall: start sacking people. As much as it made sense on paper, I just couldn't bring myself to do it. We had built a quality team and the thought of letting any of them go – many of whom were like family – was a harrowing option. Apart from putting people out in the cold at a time when there were few jobs around, such drastic action would certainly have left our remaining workforce demoralised and unsettled.

I also saw that the first people to be sacked would be the younger ones we had brought into the business, who we wanted to shape and build the business around. So sacking them may have reduced our overheads in the short term, but it would have stopped us growing the business in the long term. In later years, many of these younger advisers became the ones we came to depend on most.

I recalled those little jars of money on the shelf when I was a kid and thought, "Why not?" Why not put my Dutch thriftiness to work and save the company with frugality? Much to the annoyance of my employees, I began to look at all expenditure, even down to our subscription to the daily *Financial Review* and other newspapers that kept us abreast of trends in the business community. When my staff protested, rightly claiming they needed to stay current on financial news, I told them to visit their local library and read the papers for free!

They thought I was joking, but I wasn't. If a family can survive a financial setback by penny-pinching, a company ought to be able to do the same thing. I'm sure my Dutch heritage took a beating in the lunch room, but even this 'tiny' expense of newspaper subscriptions added up to more than $3,000 a year.

Little by little, we began to win this race. I'll never forget the time a superannuation fund manager's face lit up when I offered to take him out to lunch. He was accustomed to salaries in the $150,000 to $300,000 range. We had earned a pretty good reputation for providing old-fashioned hospitality when dining our key supporters, so you can imagine his obvious disappointment when I pulled my car into the parking lot of a sandwich café filled with pensioners. Instead of the expected medium-rare T-bone and an expensive bottle of wine at one of Hobart's five-star restaurants, I ordered toasted ham and tomato sandwiches and a bottle of water.

There was no way I was going to let our company go under.

In addition to asking our people to drastically cut their expenses, Tim and I reduced our salaries by thirty per cent and asked our other executives to do the same. Remarkably, all agreed and as a result, we never had to fire or reduce the pay of our lower-level employees.

Beneath the veneer of success

I had taken out a first and then a second mortgage on our home and took out personal loans to make up for the shortfalls in my income. Things were so grim I was forced to extend my personal credit cards to the limit. Because of my self-induced lower salary, I was barely making enough to service the interest on these debts, and despite being the CEO of a major financial services company, the loan repayments meant that for a period I was effectively the lowest-paid employee in the entire company!

On the surface, things looked pretty good. But despite all the hard work and sacrifices, the reality was that what I owed was greater than what I owned.

My wake-up call

And then it happened. It was early one morning and I was driving from our home in Hobart to Launceston – a 220 kilometre trek.

I left Hobart at 5:45 a.m., and after a tense drive crossing Tasmania's midlands where I'd negotiated fog and black ice, my mind started drifting. Having made this trip countless times, I was driving on 'autopilot,' confident that I knew the road.

About thirty kilometres out of Launceston, I rounded a bend at 110 km per hour, to discover road workers had moved the highway ten metres to my left! I'd been so absorbed in my own thoughts that I'd missed a new road sign advising motorists to slow down and found myself heading straight for a slow moving truck on my side of the road.

"This is it!" I thought, as the truck loomed ahead of me. I honestly believed I was a dead man. Out of desperation, I wrenched the steering wheel as hard as I could and in a split second amazingly I only slightly sideswiped and bounced off the side of the oncoming truck, and came to a stop fifty metres further down the road – with just minor damage to my car.

I sat there frozen in total shock, barely able to breathe. After what seemed like several minutes, I slowly eased the car back onto the road and made it safely to Launceston. Later that night, as I crawled into bed, I felt as if my life had been miraculously given back to me. I was quite shaken up by it, and couldn't get out of my mind two recurring thoughts: one, I needed to make some changes in my life and two, someone was looking after me. Sure, it could have been just plain old luck that enabled me to escape with my life, but I couldn't shake the thought that I had been protected for some special purpose, just like my father had been some forty years before.

Facing your own mortality

My father had joined the Dutch merchant navy in 1939 as a Morse code operator on missions between Europe, America and the West Indies. He was always meticulously prepared and spent his entire time in the navy with a wad of American dollars shoved down his sock and his passport around his neck. It was a habit that eventually paid dividends. His ship, the SS Haulerwijk, was sunk by a German submarine at night on its way across the North Atlantic Ocean, leaving my father and a few other survivors adrift in a lifeboat for days. Some died and had to be pushed overboard. Eventually, an American destroyer called "Rodney" picked up the surviving sailors and took them to Cape Town where my father, the only person with a passport to verify who they were to the officials and still with money in his sock, put them up in a hotel for a few days until they re-joined their own navy.

After more risky trips between Indonesia and the west coast of the USA he heard that a ship he'd previously been assigned to had been torpedoed by a Japanese submarine and that the surviving crew were beheaded! Dad was so thankful to the US President, Franklin Roosevelt and the war ship which saved him that he named his last two children in their honour, my sister was named Eleanore after Franklin Roosevelt's wife and he named my youngest brother Franklin Rodney. After that near-death experience, my father always said he knew that someone was looking after him.

There's nothing like the frightening reality of your own mortality to get your attention. My early morning accident shook me to the core, causing me to take a long, hard look at my life. I was living the dream that most men aspire to but it was quickly turning into a nightmare and I didn't have a clue what to do about it. But I was about to find out.

From the unlikeliest of sources.

**" THE BEST WAY TO
FIND YOURSELF IS TO LOSE
YOURSELF IN THE SERVICE
OF OTHERS. "**

– Mohandas K. Gandhi

6 What am I here for?

One of the biggest questions that plagues mankind is the meaning of life – to quote Hamlet – "to be or not to be?" Philosophers, politicians, artists and people all over the globe carry this same internal conundrum: Why are we here? What's the point to life? Is my life meaningless? You don't have to look far in our popular culture to see that this question is constantly being asked, but to what success? Movies like *The Karate Kid, The Matrix, Bruce Almighty* and *The Bucket List*, all centre on this age-old question but, disappointingly (yet not unexpectedly), still do not provide satisfying or definite answers.

There seems to be an underlying need in humankind that isn't satisfied with simply just 'doing life.' This feeling is humorously explored in the 1990 popular film, *Groundhog Day*. Bill Murray plays an unlikeable middle-aged man who, through some mystical force, is made to repeat the exact same day over and over again. He wakes up to the same song on the radio, drinks the same cup of coffee and delivers the same weather report at his job as a news reporter.

As I watched this movie, I felt an uncomfortable sense of familiarity to my own life; each morning I got up, showered, dressed, ate breakfast, went to work, made money, drove home, had dinner, then worked some more and went to bed. I was trapped in my own Groundhog Day.

The frightening reality staring me in the face was that when it came to what really mattered, I had very little. My life lacked real purpose and meaning. I felt as if I were on a treadmill, running hard going nowhere.

Every day I did the same thing. And the next day. And the next.

I thought if I just tried harder and got our debt under control and somehow made more money, I could finally ease up a bit, pay more attention to my family, and everything would come right. But I never seemed to reach that destination and resigned myself to thinking this was as good as it will ever get.

As I already mentioned, I had been raised a Christian and had been attending church for a long time. But as a businessman I struggled to fit into the church environment. Some of its teaching made me feel it was sinful to enjoy making money. Like so many men of my generation, I became a 'Sunday Christian,' doing just enough church to look good, but staying on the fringes and pretty much ignoring it during the week. To be painfully honest, I did my best to ignore it on Sunday as well, letting my mind drift during the message to mentally solve problems at work and make plans for the coming week. Religion for me was just another box I checked on my to-do list.

The Harley-riding preacher

It was in this mindset that I woke up one Sunday morning and seriously considered getting the family to go to church without me while I headed for the golf course. After all, the fresh air and exercise would do me some good, I was pretty much working six days a week and felt I deserved some down time just to clear my head. Instead, I shepherded everyone into the car and in a few minutes found myself unable to daydream my way through the message. And it wasn't just because the preacher – a guest speaker – sported a full beard, long hair, black leather jacket, and had ridden in on a Harley Davidson. It was what he had to say that got my full attention.

The church was full that Sunday, but John Smith's words shot straight to my heart.

His basic message was one that I had been living but couldn't quite see its futility: material wealth and the quest for success never fully satisfy the deep longing of our hearts. As a consequence, we keep trying to apply band-aid solutions to issues that are far worse than just skin deep.

Now, I had heard this song before but this leather-clad bikie guy put a new twist on this familiar tune. Instead of disparaging wealth and making me feel guilty because I had made some money, he challenged people like me to use our affluence not solely for our own comfort, but to help others. He explained that each of us had been uniquely wired and created for a greater purpose than just aiming to live a comfortable life.

In other words, I was not created by mistake, nor was I the product of some cosmic accident, as many believe. It was with a heavy heart that I pondered this truth: I was put on this earth to accomplish something for a higher purpose, yet I was living as if I were the only one who mattered.

Images of millions less fortunate flashed before my eyes as two questions echoed inside my brain: "Why am I so blessed in comparison to others? How am I going to use my life for the greater good?"

Sure, I had always planned to be generous and give money to worthwhile philanthropic causes once I made my millions, but what was I going to do in the meantime? What did I have now that could benefit others?

I didn't want to admit it, but up until now, my 'greater purpose' was trying to live a comfortable life. It wasn't intentional – I didn't write it down on a post-it note and stick it on my mirror, but by default, this had become the slogan of my life. No wonder I wasn't feeling good about myself.

According to this leather-clad bikey, my definition of wealth needed to be challenged: Wealth was limiting, rather than freeing; a liability instead of an asset; and had become a source of hurt, frustration and alienation in contrast to the potential it had to contribute to the benefit of my family and so many more.

Juggling priorities

Here's the part of his message that really hit a raw nerve: "If you want God to bless you, that will only happen when you put him first in your life." I had heard that before but hearing it from a guy who looked so out of place in church really grabbed my attention. That, plus the fact that I had become increasingly frustrated despite my material success. It was as if he had been walking around in my shoes for the past few years.

It was crystal clear that I was juggling a whole bunch of different priorities in my life, and was becoming exhausted from trying to keep all the balls in the air at the same time. And it also struck me that I had no clear overall priority or sense of destiny or purpose. I didn't have one thing that was more important than the others. As a result there wasn't that one thread to my life that connected all the other components. Was it God or money or career or success or family? What was the most important?

I came to realise that I had in fact been boxing God in. According to this bikie, I would never find the life I was created to enjoy until I not only let God out of the box, but gave him priority over everything. If I made him the centre of my life instead of myself, I would discover meaning and purpose that transcended the fleeting pleasure I got from making money. From this point on, not only did wealth start to take on a whole new meaning, I began to get more clarity surrounding my priorities and life direction.

Counter-culture thinking

Allowing this bearded bikie's message to get through my defences became the defining moment in my life. It was with amazing clarity, as if I heard an almost audible voice whisper in my head: "John, I didn't create you to be successful. I created you to help other people to be successful and by doing that you will become truly successful".

My heart began racing. It was as if the lights went on in my life with dazzling brilliance. As the preacher spoke I felt an overwhelming sense of transformation. For years my head and my heart had been wrestling as I searched for my life's purpose, then suddenly it all seemed crystal clear! In an instant, things I wanted to do moved from my head into my heart. I felt God's love touch deep inside me in a way I'd not felt before. A sense of real peace came over my heart as the weight of 'success' began to crumble. From that point on, I knew life was going to move forward in a positive way because for the first time in my life I had taken myself out of the equation. My life wasn't about me – it was about helping others.

I raced home from church, went into my study, shut the door and started writing a list of the things that I needed to change in my life before I forgot. I didn't have to think about what needed to change. I just wrote it all down. It was as if I was transcribing what was being dictated to me.

Not to be overly dramatic, but I honestly felt my very life was at stake. In many different ways it was, and it started with putting at risk the relationships I valued the most; and I could not contemplate life without Sue or my children.

Thirteen things to change

By the time I had finished writing, I had a list of thirteen ways I needed to change:

1 Make myself available for community work – no more excuses.

2 Stop making decisions based solely on what I wanted. Instead, make decisions that are in keeping with my new purpose of helping others succeed.

3 Begin to read the Bible as though it were written personally for me.

4 Make it a priority to spend more time with my wife, children and friends and stop using my busyness, my business, or my headaches as an excuse.

5 Apply Christian principles to my business and implement the practical truths of my faith.

6 Be prepared to make a fool of myself in pursuing what I know to be right. Do not trust only my own ability, but trust God more and be more open about my faith.

7 Stop chasing success and pursue purpose instead.

8 Dream more. Follow my dreams even if others think they're stupid.

9 Be kind to myself. Take the time to look after myself and do the things I enjoy.

10 Take more risks and become more radical.

11 Be honest about my weaknesses but don't concentrate on them. Let others cover my weaknesses while I concentrate on my strengths.

12 Accept pain and make the hard decisions. Don't avoid healthy conflict.

13 Don't be competitive just for the sake of winning.

Change or die

A few years ago, Alan Deutschman wrote a book with the provocative title, *Change or Die*. Its premise is based on this question the author poses: "What if a well-informed, trusted authority figure said you had to make difficult and enduring changes in the way you think, feel and act? If you didn't, your time would end soon – a lot sooner than it had to. Could you alter your life when it mattered most?"

I knew I had to alter my life, but on the surface the change I needed to make just didn't make sense: to help yourself you must help others. I had to admit that my way wasn't working. I had been pouring myself into my work to improve my own life, but I was miserable. As the bikie preacher spoke, I came to a rather shocking conclusion that if I continued living the way I was, I would probably lose my family, my health and most likely die with a lot of money and the bitterness of knowing I had lived my life in vain.

It really was a 'change or die' moment.

Entering halftime

I didn't realise it at the time, but I was entering what author Bob Buford calls "Halftime". (Click on www.halftime.org.au if you would like more details.) The first half of my career was all about gaining, achieving, acquiring. It is not necessarily a bad thing, but more often than not it will never deliver everything you think it will, and eventually you reach a point where you know you can't continue pushing the rock up the hill. Like an athlete who just played a difficult first half, it was time for me to go into the change rooms and adjust my game plan – halftime. Halftime is a pause sometime after the first half of your life – at midlife – to look back and take stock, then to look forward and dream and chart a course for your second half.

My halftime experience began with an increasing level of frustration that something was wrong and that I had to make changes. That growing sense of discontent allowed me to catch a glimpse of what my life needed to become, and gave me the resolve to make the changes to realign and recalibrate my life.

Quite literally, I was redefining what it meant to be 'wealthy'. Over time, these changes would profoundly transform me from being success-driven yet unfulfilled, to a life where increasingly I found meaning and purpose.

My list of things that I had to change in my life was not necessarily profound or revolutionary. I did not decide to become a missionary or sell everything and give all the proceeds to the poor. I had been wired in such a way that enabled me to create wealth and I didn't think I was expected to turn my back on my God given gift.

I had found my life-purpose

The reason I was so unfulfilled was that I was building my business for *myself.*

Thanks to an unconventional preacher, I was able to shift my purpose away from myself and redirect it towards others. Those thirteen changes would help me to focus on my new 'life-purpose,' which simply stated is to help other people succeed. That would now become the true measure of my success.

I once worked closely with a businessman who was extremely talented. A marketing genius. He was the kind of guy who seemed to be able to accomplish anything, and he poured himself into his work and delivered fantastic results. But he was so focused on success that in the end, sadly he not only lost his marriage, but died chasing what he could never quite grasp.

That could just as easily have been me, were it not for the revelation I experienced in church. Identifying the things I needed to change was an important first step, but as I've learned so often in business, it's one thing to create a plan but quite another to implement it.

Would I really be able to change the trajectory of my life and regain all that was truly important to me?

It didn't take long before I was put to the test.

" IT IS ONE OF THE MOST BEAUTIFUL COMPENSATIONS OF THIS LIFE THAT NO MAN CAN SINCERELY TRY TO HELP ANOTHER WITHOUT HELPING HIMSELF. **"**

– Ralph Waldo Emerson

7 Paradigm shift

It's not that I didn't want to help people.

Over the years I had done a little volunteer work and
I did enjoy it. But I was just too busy to be intentional about
it. In many ways, my 'philanthropy' was a bit like church
for me – I actually believed in it, but it was just another box
on a menu of items that I regularly ticked by making a small
donation here and there. I just didn't have time for these
'distractions' at this stage in my life.

A few years ago, Ken Robinson, one of the world's leading
authorities on leadership wrote an intriguing book, *The
Element: How Finding Your Passion Changes Everything* in
which he encourages readers to combine their talents
with something they are passionate about. It was clear
I had a talent for business-building, motivating people
and finding creative solutions to problems. But I can't say
I was all that passionate about anything. I found a certain

degree of satisfaction in doing deals and seeing people in my company grow, but work for me was more of a means to an end, and the end was always about becoming more successful.

But the bikie preacher ignited something inside of me that made me do something outrageous – at least for me.

Getting my life back

Shortly after I penned the list of thirteen things I wanted to change in my life my close friend, Klaas Laning, who was a board member of my children's private school, called and asked me if I would volunteer to become the school's treasurer. I listened as he went on to explain the school was in serious financial trouble – losing hundreds of thousands of dollars a year – and the current treasurer had just resigned. He said the board was looking for someone outside of school management to take the financial reins and steer it out of trouble.

On the one hand I had a soft spot for this school as its founding fathers included my own parents and an uncle. Not only had I been a student there, albeit briefly as the school opened when I entered grade six, but I had seen the sacrifices my parents had made so that their kids could attend a school that taught values as well as the Three Rs. And, of course, my own children attended this school, which had now fallen into serious financial trouble.

But trying to fix this school that I loved just didn't make sense to me. I already had a business to run that consumed most of my waking hours. I didn't relish making the tough decisions I would have to make to get the school back in the black. And the whole world of education seemed like a planet way outside my galaxy. Besides, there were the headaches. I was certain that adding more stress to my life would make them worse. The last thing I needed was to add more work and stress to my life.

Even as I stared at my mental list of reasons to say no, I knew this was exactly what John Smith, the preacher, was talking about. I was being offered a cause; a reason to really live life rather than just keep slogging away on the treadmill. I had spent my entire adult life focused on my career, and where had it got me? Becoming treasurer of a private school in financial trouble didn't make sense, but making sense was quickly losing its appeal.

So I agreed to become the treasurer of the school.

'Buyer's remorse' set in almost immediately. I'd never been big on business analysis and research, and I possessed an almost desperate fear of public speaking – two things at the top of my new job description. Maybe I should have told them "no" after all. But even as I dived into the stacks of financial records, I felt something I hadn't felt in some time: excitement.

If I could just work out where the problems were, I thought, the school would survive and a lot of people would be relieved. Instead of breaking my back for my own gain, I was doing something that would pay huge dividends for generations, and I had to admit that felt pretty good.

As it turned out, I didn't need to be an expert analyst to discover why the school was in such bad shape: our fees were significantly lower than the nation's average for similar private schools. Over the years, expenses outpaced income, but the school stubbornly refused to sufficiently raise its fees due to the fear of a parental revolt! The solution was pretty clear. If we raised the fees by fifty per cent, we could operate a sustainable enterprise.

Guess whose job it was to present this solution to the parents enjoying our bargain fee structure?

I swallowed back my fear of public speaking and made my presentation to two hundred stunned parents. As I went over the numbers and referred to the charts and graphs I had prepared, not once did I experience the racing heartbeat and sweaty palms that accompanied me on the rare occasion I had to speak in public. I knew it was because

I was contributing to something worthwhile that I had the courage to speak easily and with confidence.

The parents almost unanimously agreed to the new fees – only one family withdrew their children. Not only did the school survive, but it prospered, taking over another school a few years later.

Doing something that matters

I've done a lot of deals for my company that made a lot of money for my employees and myself, but none of those deals gave me the satisfaction I got in helping this school. To know that my efforts played a role in allowing children to receive a faith-based education for generations to come fuelled a growing passion that I had never felt before.

It may have done something else, too.

As predicted, trying to save the school added about twenty hours per week to the eighty hours I devoted to my business, so I decided to cut back on the hours I spent with my business. Still, twenty hours of painstaking work pushed me out of my comfort zone, and despite the relief from my business, I was still putting in ridiculously long days. The time spent working for the school put me in a different headspace that left me feeling refreshed and more alive than ever. Instead of being the grumpy father and husband who retreated to his room after a day at the office, I returned home happier than ever. I had found something to apply my talents to that replenished me, rather than sucking out all that I had to give.

I began spending more time with my family, not so much out of obligation to my commitment to change, but because something indeed was happening inside me. I felt useful. By focusing on others I began to see myself in a new light – someone with value beyond what can be measured on a spreadsheet. I recalled the verse that John Smith quoted that Sunday: "What good will it be for a man if he gains the whole world, yet forfeits his own soul?"

Gradually, as I poured myself into the school's financial troubles, I began to get my life back. I made it a priority to spend as much time with Sue as possible, discovering all over again why I was so attracted to her. I was also sleeping better, which I'm sure contributed to my general sense of well-being. And with the help of a naturopath and my new-found sense of mission, my headaches thankfully eased up.

Helping others succeed

Meanwhile, my work in the business improved as well. Despite substantially cutting back my time at the office, I was just as productive. Less pressure and a more positive outlook on life made me a better leader. I was more insightful, I could make decisions faster and I had regained the creativity that had become dulled by indifference and emotional fatigue.

Something in my life returned that had been missing for a long time: purpose – purpose that mattered. As Bob Buford so succinctly described it, I was embarking on a journey from success to significance, and loving every minute of it. Over the next few years, I would lend my skills to other causes which produced the same results: success for others, which brought a great deal of joy and soul-satisfying pleasure to me.

Whilst I am still very busy, it's from doing what I was created to do and my life feels significantly more enriched as a result. I have become much more discerning about how many things I want to juggle and whether they are focused on enriching other people's lives.

Having an enriched existence is not necessarily about slowing down or working less. Very simply, it's all about shifting the focus of your life from yourself to others.

Part 2 An Enriched Life

Enriched – 1. to supply with abundance of anything desirable.
2. to make finer in quality as by supplying desirable elements
or ingredients. 3. to enhance, make finer in flavour, colour,
or significance.

– Macquarie Dictionary

" WEALTH AND HAPPINESS IS NEVER OBTAINED WHEN SOUGHT AFTER DIRECTLY. IT COMES AS A BYPRODUCT OF PROVIDING A USEFUL SERVICE. "

– Ralph Waldo Emerson

8 Glimpses of an enriched life

A modern fable

An investment banker from Sydney was driving through rural Queensland when he came upon a roadside stand where a man was selling fruit and vegetables. It was around lunchtime so he stopped to buy some strawberries. He couldn't believe both the variety and quality of the produce, and complimented the man running the stand.

"You know, I could help you expand your business," he continued.

"Really?" the farmer replied. "How would that work?"

"Well, I could help you get a small-business loan so that you could buy more land to increase your production. Then you could hire a trucking company to deliver your produce to the markets in Sydney and Melbourne where you'll get a better price. Each year you could grow a little more, hire workers to help you, maybe even buy your own trucks to take your produce to the markets. Eventually you could sell your business and have enough money so you'd never have to work again."

"How long would that take?" the farmer asked.

"With a little luck and a lot of hard work, maybe about twenty years."

The farmer thought for a few moments and then asked, "Why would I want to do that?"

"Because then you would have more time to spend with your family, enjoy life a little, and do all those things you've always wanted to do but never had time for."

"Well mate," the farmer replied. "I don't make much money, but I love working the land and then selling what I'm able to grow. I suppose I could work longer and harder and make more money, but then I wouldn't be able to sit on the verandah with my missus like we do every night, watching the sun go down. I wouldn't be able to help my kids with their schoolwork in the afternoon or volunteer like I do with our local fire brigade. The way I see it, I can save myself twenty years of misery by just doing what I'm doing and I still get all the benefits your plan would give me."

The investment banker paid for his fruit, got back into his car, and drove off with a lot to think about.

By just about every standard, that poor farmer had not achieved wealth and success. He didn't even own a suit; he drove a worn-out old truck. But even though he probably couldn't define it, he had something everyone eventually wants: an enriched existence.

Driven to succeed

I'm not suggesting you set aside your ambitions and goals and go and live off the land. When my schedule gets too full, I sometimes think wistfully of my carefree working holiday days and wonder if I could still be content bouncing around from job to job and living the simple life. But even though there are people who do just that, most of us are wired to build and add value, and there's nothing wrong with that. Despite the toll it took on me, I enjoyed the privilege of being able to provide good jobs for my employees that helped them pay for houses, cars and education costs. An industrious, entrepreneurial spirit helps build prosperous societies.

It's just that when most of us start out, we're not really thinking about things like purpose and meaning. As true 'hunter-gatherers' we're driven to succeed and create wealth; to climb the ladder and provide our families with the things we may not have had when we were young. We want to 'make it', but at some point along the way – whether we reach all of our career goals or not – 'making it' takes on a new meaning. Somewhere, deep within, a voice whispers into our hearts: "Is this really what I want to do for the rest of my life?"

It's a question that led Ian Learnmouth to leave his job as executive director of *Macquarie Bank* and move into the social/not-for-profit sector. He said, "I had already been working for twenty years in the corporate world and I asked myself, 'Do I want to make it thirty-five?'" He went on to say that moving into the social sector allowed him to "connect his head to his heart."

Connecting 'head to heart' is a good place to start if you are dissatisfied with solely the pursuit of more wealth and success, and a more enriched life is what you are yearning for. It suggests a marriage between the skills and abilities you've been given and those you are most passionate about. Going back to my childhood days when I collected and sold golf balls, I developed a talent for sales and then for managing the money I earned from selling them. When I finally settled down to start my career, these were the skills I used to build a successful business.

For a few years or so, my head was in the game, but not my

heart. But it didn't matter. I was building a business and didn't think much about things like purpose and meaning.

Eventually though, we all reach a point where making more money, getting another promotion or acquiring another company no longer gives us the thrill it once did. What we really want is to know that what we are doing matters. And in most cases, we come to the frightening reality that it doesn't – that while all we've accomplished is commendable and allows us to enjoy enviable lifestyles, it doesn't quite deliver the contentment we once thought it would.

What will outlive you?

According to a great teacher, the only wealth that offers any lasting value is one that is invested in something bigger than yourself. In one of his most confronting and challenging teachings, Jesus urged his followers to not grasp for and store up treasures just for themselves on earth, which moth and rust would destroy and thieves could break in and steal. Instead, Jesus told his followers to store up for themselves treasures in heaven. He then went on to say that where your treasure is, there your heart will be.

Even if you are not a religious person, this advice makes perfect sense when you stop to think about it. All that hard work to buy stuff that you have to work even harder to take care of is the ultimate treadmill, which leads nowhere. One day, all that you have built will either be destroyed or become someone else's. You only really have it for a little while. That's where leaving a legacy comes in.

Legacy is the one thing that doesn't disappear after you die and it's also something that inspires and helps people long after you're able to. I'm not talking about putting a plaque on a park bench by a nice river or giving your antique collection to a museum – although there is nothing wrong with these things.

Gifts like these are extremely generous and have undoubtedly touched the lives of millions of people but not all of us have the funds to leave behind such a hefty will to the general public. That's okay. A legacy isn't about the amount you leave behind but the impact you have on other people's lives.

Impacting future generations

Recently, I was very moved by the legacy left by one well-known Irish-born Australian, a man by the name of Jim Stynes. After a debilitating battle with cancer, he died at the age of 45. In his younger days he was best known as a top Australian Rules football player, the only non Australian born AFL player to win the prestigious

Brownlow Medal, which he won in 1991. Subsequently, he was inducted into the Australian Hall of Fame. From the time of his entry into the Australian Football League in 1987, right up until his retirement in 1998, Stynes played a league record of 244 consecutive games and was famous for his added strengths of being an exceptional endurance athlete with an unusual but very accurate kicking action. Following his extraordinarily successful football career, Stynes began to focus on youth work and used his public profile to launch the *Reach Foundation* – an organisation aimed at helping to motivate disadvantaged children to achieve their dreams. As a result of his work with young people he was twice named *Victorian of the Year*, in 2001 and 2003, and with the expanded profile of Reach nationally, was awarded the *Medal of the Order of Australia* in 2007.

When Jim was first diagnosed with a terminal illness in July 2009 and told he had less than a year to live, the news was surprising. He was only forty-two years old and was fit and healthy, not to mention a devoted husband and loving father to two primary school-aged children. He knew his odds weren't good, but with so much to lose Jim put everything he had into trying to beat the disease.

Unfortunately, three years later Jim died, but his legacy lives on in the hearts of many thousands of Australians.

In a truly touching gesture, the Australian Prime Minister recently announced thirty-seven scholarships – Stynes' playing number – for disadvantaged young people from indigenous or multicultural backgrounds as a memorial to Stynes and to celebrate his life-changing work with young people nationwide.

Jim Stynes is a clear example of a success story that became an enriched life as he transformed his early success as a sporting star into an enduring legacy by using his influence to create something of lasting value for others. He invested in something bigger than himself – and his legacy will live on and impact generations to come.

We can't all win awards and have scholarships named after us, but hopefully Jim's story illustrates how someone can integrate their first half success into a second half that helps others.

Jim's story makes me wonder what my legacy will be? Maybe when you reflect on this you are not sure. If so take a minute to ask yourself how much of your time and energy you invest purposefully in others in a way that will outlive you and leave a lasting impact. This legacy is far greater than the money and material assets you can accumulate and leave for your loved ones – it's all about living a life that matters.

In theory, that may sound good, but how do you actually do it? How do you find that passion for something beyond your own self-interests, and once you finally discover it, what do you do next? From my own experience, and from working with others to help them on a similar journey, here are five suggestions to get you started.

1 Know what makes you tick

Finding your life's purpose is more than just looking over a list of not-for-profit organisations and then picking one to support. It's an investment of your time, talent (skills) and treasure (resources) into something that connects with your core values.

For me, it was my Christian faith. If you are not a religious person, your core values might be related to a particular cause such as human rights or improving the state education system. One way to get going is to ask yourself, "What do I care about so deeply that I would risk my life for it?"

Here's another approach. To get our teenage children to start thinking about their purpose I used to ask them, "What annoys you most in the world or what upsets you?" Chances are this same grievance is actually a passion.

In the movie *City Slickers*, the characters played by Jack Palance and Billy Crystal had a short but very crucial conversation about life's purpose. In it, Jack intimated to Billy that the key to finding one's true purpose in life is to discover the 'one thing' that stands out and makes everything else secondary. Billy then asked what the 'one thing' was, to which Jack responded, "It's different for everyone." Many people have latched onto the idea of discovering their 'one thing' which can then be the catalyst to personal life transformation that subsequently impacts entire communities and societies.

Seriously, I believe that if you can't point to that 'one thing' that is the driving force in your life, you will have a very difficult time finding your life's real purpose, so give yourself the time and space to understand what really matters to you.

For example, it really annoyed my wife and I that the local school our kids attended and the church we belonged to were not functioning properly. I soon realised this discontent was actually linked to my passion and when combined with my skills, I was able to help restructure these organisations so they could be more successful and reach their full potential.

If necessary, take a personal retreat and focus on this question, "Aside from my family and my career, what do I value most?"

2 Look around

I know it sounds simplistic, but it's amazing how we can get so caught up and preoccupied with our own little universe that we fail to see what's going on in the rest of the world.

Recently, there was a successful executive in the United States who felt a growing passion to invest his time and energy to help young people but didn't know where to start. Then, one day he noticed his office was a few blocks away from one of the worst public schools in his city, and that's when the light went on in his head. He had probably walked past that school hundreds of times but never really noticed it. He decided to roll up his sleeves and get involved. He made a big impact turning it into one of the best schools in the city. Once you determine your 'one thing', you'll see things that once escaped your view.

3 Instead of "no way", think "why not?"

If you listen to your passions and begin to explore opportunities to focus on your 'one thing', you will most likely come up with some pretty audacious plans but think, "I could never do that." Many people miss the chance to enrich their lives because they close the door on it.

A few years ago, I took Sue to see the film, *Yes Man*, starring Jim Carrey. The movie had an interesting storyline which caught my attention. In it, Jim Carrey plays a negative, miserly no-hoper who through a series of events, decides to say "Yes" to every offer and opportunity that comes his way. While it landed him in some pretty questionable situations, on the whole, his life was transformed and he was a new, happier version of himself. He won back his old friends who had disowned him, scored a job promotion and of course, got the girl of his dreams. Now, I'm not suggesting you say "yes" to *every* situation that presents itself to you, but there is a certain attractiveness about people who have a positive, can-do approach in life; especially, when it comes from those in high positions of power and authority.

I almost missed an opportunity when board members from the private school asked me to help them because my initial thought was "absolutely not!" Like me, you can come up with a dozen sound reasons why you shouldn't take that first step, or you can jump in with the same reckless enthusiasm that helped you become a success in your career.

At Garrisons, the financial services company I built, many people told me "no way, it can't be done." A well-meaning, high-level executive from Sydney said, "Why try and build an Australia-wide financial planning business from a remote island and in a small city like Hobart? It will be too hard." If I had listened to this 'wisdom', the company would never have been the success that it became. Similarly, I heard "no way" about our plans to sell the offices we owned to the financial planners in those offices. I heard "no way" to the idea of then franchising those offices. I heard "no way" when I wanted to start our own funds management company, *Synergy Capital Management*. Over the eight years from the time that I said "why not" to these things, to the time that we sold Garrisons, we grew from five offices to approximately sixty-five and also built Synergy into a highly successful and profitable funds management company.

So when some of my friends said "no way" when they heard about my new purpose and mission in life, I ignored them. Had I listened to them, I'd still be stuck on the success treadmill.

4 Start small – so you can test it out

In the euphoria of discovering my new sense of mission and devotion to a cause, it would have been tempting to try and save the world by starting a massive charitable organisation. And it would have been a mistake. I knew how to run a business, but I had a lot to learn about 'saving the world,' and helping my private school was a great first step in the learning process. It helped me overcome my fear of public speaking and taught me how to lead by persuasion and vision-casting, instead of relying on a position of authority.

On a practical level, it allowed me to continue in my career while testing the waters of the social sector – what author Bob Buford calls a "parallel career."

5 Stick with it

Many of my clients get excited about their new philanthropic adventures but once the shininess has worn off, they jump ship. This happened to someone I used to coach. He got involved in an incredible literacy for adults program and made a huge impact on the not-for-profit organisation that was operating this service to the community. However, like an excitable kid besotted by a new Christmas present, once the shiny newness wore off, he got bored. He was so interested in the 'buzz' *he* got, he forgot about those he was actually helping! He may have helped the organisation at first, but without his continued leadership, it quickly had to abandon many of the ideas and structures he had implemented in the first place.

A lot of people who take that initial step towards living an enriched life return to their original lives because they just cannot escape the gravitational pull of their own personal success. The transition from success to living an enriched life initially requires some discipline to keep us from falling back into the rut. Even as you start small, continue looking around for other opportunities to make a deposit into that 'one thing' that makes you tick. It wasn't long after I had helped the private school get back on track that another opportunity related to my faith presented itself. This time it was the church we belonged to that was really struggling. When the eldership board heard how I had helped the school, they asked me to do the same for the church! Again, my first reaction was to come up with a list of reasons why I wasn't up for the challenge. But my growing spirit of reckless abandonment to a cause bigger than me won out, and I jumped in, as they say, with both feet.

I'm no theologian and certainly not a Bible scholar, but for the first three months I met weekly with the leadership team of the church and using the Bible as our guide, I put together a document outlining the purpose of the church. Then we developed a strategic plan to help the church live out that purpose. In essence, I was using the skills I had gained as a business leader to help the church do a better job of serving our community.

The fact that church attendance rose from three hundred to six hundred, and annual giving soared from $120,000 to $400,000 was personally satisfying, but more importantly, it affirmed for me that I was moving in the right direction. I really could connect my beliefs and values with my passion for helping people and organisations reach their full potential. I probably couldn't have described it at the time, but I was slowly being weaned from mere success as I discovered the richer rewards of significance.

I was still heavily engaged in my business but these two small steps, involving the school and the church, were intoxicating and spurred me further along on the journey to enrichment. So much so, that I found myself eagerly awaiting another dose of this powerful drug.

I didn't have to wait very long, and this time I got completely hooked!

Before you move to the next chapter, consider these two questions:

1 *What makes you tick? List at least five things that are vitally important to you.*

2 *What things can you see around you that are crying out for **your** help?*

" IF MAN HASN'T DISCOVERED SOMETHING TO DIE FOR, HE ISN'T FIT TO LIVE. "

– Martin Luther King

9 Finding your life purpose

Today, finding one's passion is an ideal infiltrating the very core of our culture. From early childhood, helping your kids find their 'one thing' is strongly encouraged, spurred on by media coverage of young child stars and sporting heroes. Recently, I saw a brochure for a kids' holiday camp, which said: "Help Your Child Find their Passion," in shiny, bold letters and it went on to list the range of 'taster' activities available. The list was mind-boggling: martial arts, musical theatre, photography, creative writing, circus skills and every sport you could possibly imagine.

Sounds great on paper, but with so many options available, it seems unlikely that any child could possibly pick just one thing to be passionate about! It's like standing in a bakery of fine desserts and only being allowed to pick one! The choices are overwhelming, and often, it's easier not to pick anything at all, or to take a small bite of many things.

For the older generation, myself included, this concept of finding one's passion is relatively new. Generally, we weren't encouraged to think about what we were passionate about – it was survival of the fittest. If you had clothes and food and a roof over your head you were doing well. And if you managed to make a decent living, that was considered living the dream.

But in my experience, finding your 'one thing' is the key to finding meaning in this life.

"But I don't know what my 'one thing' is", I can hear you saying in frustration. That's okay. Neither did I for a long time. It's not necessarily something that we are born with.

For most people, the journey involves a series of side-trips that guide them to discover what they are most passionate about – an irresistible cause or mission that captures their heart and soul and won't let go.

Walk before you run

After my defining moment that Sunday morning, I had my own series of side-trips before I ran towards my 'one thing.' As much as I enjoyed helping not-for-profits get back in the game, I wasn't quite ready to quit my day job.

Chances are the thought of abandoning ship and jumping into your 'one thing' probably seems a bit scary. But that's okay, it is for most of us. It's a process.

To be honest, during my earlier transitional stage, I still loved running my business – maybe even more than ever before, once I had my priorities straight. The stress-induced headaches that had plagued me had significantly reduced in their severity, our marriage was back on the right path, and I was able to carve out time to spend with the kids. I didn't recognise it at the time, but that period was part of the weaning process.

In my experience, even once you've identified your 'one thing', there is a time of transition which for me and for most people might take quite a few years. In hindsight, after my defining moment it probably took me about another ten years to make the complete transition. I had a parallel career for all that time, where I spent seventy-five per cent of my time still in business and twenty-five per cent in the not-for-profit area.

During this transitional time, one of the first things I had to do was break my addiction to success – and that was not easy! While I was starting to put my skills and passions to good use in the community, my company continued to grow in leaps and bounds. We had reached our goal of becoming the premier financial planning firm in Tasmania, so my entrepreneurial drive made it a natural and logical step to set my sights on the rest of Australia.

Perfect timing

The ambitious strategic plan that Tim and I had worked on closely now had a momentum all of its own. Over the next few years we began a quiet assault on the financial services giants in Australia. In four years we grew from five offices to sixty-five and became a major presence around most of Australia, with offices in the cities, country towns and fringe metropolitan areas in Victoria, South Australia, New South Wales and Queensland, as well as Tasmania. It wasn't long before our success attracted the attention of others, and with it a couple of offers to buy the company.

One of the offers was just too good to turn down and the timing was perfect. Our vision for the business was close to being achieved and both Tim and I felt clearly we were ready to step over the threshold of success into our respective second-half careers. Pretty soon after, I found myself standing in a sea of suits in a Sydney office signing ninety-seven different legal agreements to lock in the deal.

As I penned my name on each of the neatly arranged papers, I glanced out of the large floor-to-ceiling windows that gave me a full panoramic view over Sydney Harbour's Opera House. It was rather a symbolic scene, given the iconic moment and I couldn't help but smile to myself. Here I was selling a $40 million business wearing a $120 suit! Who said Dutch frugality didn't pay off? It was one of those surreal moments where you feel like you are hovering above yourself, watching the scene below.

As I celebrated that night with Sue and the kids, I couldn't help but think that only a few years earlier my family relationships were hanging by mere threads, the business was crippled by debt making big monthly losses and I was suffering the effect of my debilitating migraines – how differently this all could have turned out.

Corporate social responsibility

Life couldn't have been better for me, but it wasn't long before it became clear that when we sold the company, we sold a bit of our soul along with it. Most of our management team were shareholders and made off with lucrative share payouts. Some started new businesses, some hopped on planes to travel the world, some reached for their fishing rods. We went from having an experienced, cohesive team dedicated to defending our culture of generosity and integrity, to an influx of individuals who seemed focused on one thing – making more money for themselves. The success that we had achieved seemed to draw others who were attracted to success. That became painfully obvious on one of our obligatory company conferences – this time at a five-star resort in Phuket, Thailand.

For days we lived it up like kings and queens at the local restaurants, bars and markets before returning each night to our five-star hotel. We bartered with the local traders, walking away with armfuls of bargains that would test our airplane baggage limits. One of our financial planners upgraded his wardrobe by having thirteen suits tailor-made for him in two days!

We had a ball, but as our bus passed by the miles of crude straw huts on the way back to the airport, a heavy wave of guilt swept over me. We'd flown into their world, had a great time, screwed down their prices, and were leaving them as we found them – in mud and poverty. These were the same people who had made our beds, opened doors for us, and scrambled to bring us food and drinks whenever we beckoned.

An almost toxic mixture of shame and indignation began to stir within me. How can I enjoy such luxury at the expense of these people who go home every night to their squalid conditions? What right do I have to take so much from them yet leave little behind? And how do I square this with my new desire to serve God by serving others?

For days after this conference I felt deflated and frustrated. I wasn't proud of what we'd become as a company, so I began challenging my colleagues to give back to the Thai people. To their credit, at the next conference together we donated more than $80,000 to build an orphanage in one of the poorest regions of Thailand. Something had begun in me that I was unable to stop.

Outside influences

It was about this time that I was introduced to the book, *Halftime*, written by Bob Buford who would later become a good friend. Bob took over his family's cable television company and built it into a very successful business. Life was good, but one day Bob received a phone call informing him that his only child, Ross, had drowned.

In his book, Bob explained that he had been stuck on the treadmill of remarkable success during the first half of his career. His son's tragic death served as a wake-up call leading him to question his laser-like focus on success. With the help of a strategic planning mentor – who happened to be an atheist – he learned that he had to make a choice regarding the driving force in his life: money and success, or God. He chose God and decided to invest his time, talent and treasure into things of eternal value. The first half of his career was all about success; the second would produce significance. As he wrote in his book, the game may be set up in the first half, but it's always won in the second half! And no matter what our first half was, we all have the opportunity to win in the second half.

Wow, I thought! This is what I want to do, but how do I do it? Where do I start?

Perhaps sensing my lack of clarity, my business partner, Tim, invited me to go to a leadership practicum he was attending in Hawaii. For some time Tim had been suggesting that I meet up with a very interesting acquaintance of his, an Indian businessman called Jossy Chacko. I had never heard of Jossy before, but quickly found out he ran one of the world's most progressive charitable organisations, *Empart*, and that he lived in Melbourne. For whatever reason, Jossy and I had never quite managed to meet, and I quickly forgot all about the Indian entrepreneur, until I found myself sitting next to him, quite by 'accident' on the ten-hour flight to Hawaii.

Getting my attention

For the next ten hours I listened to Jossy as he told his remarkable story. You can read it for yourself in his book *Madness*, but the part that really got my attention was his transition from living life as a successful businessman to a full-time social entrepreneur.

Jossy had moved to Australia from South India at the age of seventeen with the aim of becoming a successful businessman. His dream was to make a lot of money fast, and at age thirty he planned to retire on his earnings and buy a hobby farm in Tasmania. It may sound far-fetched, but when he and his wife met some years later, he was rapidly climbing the corporate ladder at a national storage distribution and logistics company and was well on his way to fulfilling his dream.

Jossy's plans veered drastically off course during his honeymoon in North India when he and his bride, Jenni, were confronted by an orphan who changed their lives forever. Raju appeared to be about eight years old, but had no idea how old he was, who his parents were, or even where he was born. He lived in a slum near the New Delhi railway station in a crude tent made with sticks, cardboard and plastic sheeting. His gaunt frame and distended belly indicated severe malnutrition, and he told Jossy that during his short life he had suffered frequent sexual abuse, witnessed a couple of murders, and had suffered broken bones on several occasions when rail guards threw him from moving trains.

Initially, Raju seemed wary of Jossy and his wife. Some of his friends had gone off with strangers and were found days later sewn up with one of their kidneys stolen, victims of India's organ thieves. Jossy was so taken by the poor boy's story that he turned to his bride and suggested they take him in for the rest of their honeymoon. Jenni readily agreed, so for the next two weeks they pampered him at the best hotels and restaurants, incredulous at the way he ordered everything on the menu as if it were his last meal.

The newlyweds quickly learned that Raju had a plan to escape his poverty. If he could save up enough money to buy a shoe cart, he could make a decent living polishing and repairing shoes. But every time he came close to the $200 needed to buy the cart, rail workers would steal his cash from its hiding place under a train track.

Jossy was struck by the fact that Raju's dreams were similar to his own childhood aspirations, and that the only difference was that Jossy had been born into a privileged family. The boy was trying, but life was beating him down. Naturally, Jossy gave Raju the $200 to buy the shoe cart, but couldn't shake the boy from his mind after returning to Melbourne.

Over several months and influenced by another trip to Northern India, Jossy gradually came to the awareness that he could not continue business as usual. In what many would call an irrational act, Jossy shelved his ambition of becoming wealthy, resigned from his lucrative position, and wrote out a business plan for a venture that would drastically improve the lives of millions of impoverished people in Northern India. In essence, he had arrived at the same place I had. Jossy knew in his heart that he needed to redefine wealth, and in doing so shift the goal-posts of his life to be in alignment with that discovery. This set him on an unstoppable journey that to date has positively impacted hundreds of thousands of lives.

I was almost disappointed when the plane touched down in Hawaii, I wanted to hear more. Jossy must have read my thoughts because as we got up to leave he said, "Why don't you come to India with me and see for yourself?"

My second half adventure begins

And so, a few short weeks later, I jumped on another plane and went with Jossy to India. Over three weeks, I saw first-hand how Jossy's new venture was transforming the lives of society's rejects. His plan was ambitious yet simple, but more importantly, it resonated with my own desire to put my faith on the line. Borrowing from the business model of the franchise, Jossy built his program around training and sending out local leaders who would serve the spiritual, physical and economic needs of people to bring about community transformation. For just $100 each, women were given a new sewing machine and trained to run their own tailoring businesses. The workers Jossy trained also opened children's homes for the orphans and scores of children abandoned by parents who could not care for them.

Coming back from India I realised I had new eyes to see what was truly of value, and what wasn't. The poverty I saw in North India, along with the admirable work Jossy's organisation was doing to help those people, changed my perceptions about what was of greater value. I wanted to be a part of something bigger and of more lasting value than just building a bigger business.

It became clear, my 'one thing' was helping other people succeed. And so far, I had achieved some success. But after my trip to India, I was ready to dive into a new venture that had nothing to do with success.

One of the ideas weighing heavily on my heart was finding ways to help business people who, like me, had lost their way. My immediate dream was to organise lunchtime gatherings of business people at a pub to talk about the challenges we faced, how to keep it all in perspective, and how to pin our lives to something deeper than financial success. I had also hoped to give them an experience like I had in India to jump-start their own thinking about reaching out to others, and that's when the light went on in my head. It occurred to me that there were thousands of business leaders throughout Australia who were trapped on the success treadmill, desperately seeking something they would never find – unless they could catch sight of what 'an enriched life' looked like for them.

The lunchtime sessions at the pub in Hobart were a success with several of my executive team and other professionals around town coming regularly. Importantly, it was a way in which I could gently put my foot in the water to test out my idea. It was a baby step on my journey. From that time, my vision and the ways in which I pursue it have grown, but that first step was necessary to catapult me into a bigger arena.

" PEOPLE NOW HAVE TWO LIVES – LIFE 1 AND LIFE 2 – AND THEY ARE OVER-PREPARED FOR LIFE 1 AND UNDER-PREPARED FOR LIFE 2 AND THERE IS NO UNIVERSITY FOR THE SECOND HALF OF LIFE. "

– Peter Drucker

10 Blueprint for life

I still love escaping to the beaches along the Gold Coast in Queensland to take my chances body-surfing against the strong waves after a storm. There's something exhilarating about swimming out into the powerful surf and then letting a wave lift and throw you back to shore. Every now and then, a rip current forms and you find yourself being carried out into the deep. Not only is it frightening, but these currents can be lethal – twenty-five per cent of all drownings along Australia's coast are attributed to rips. What happens is that people caught in these currents do what seems to make sense – they instinctively swim against the current as hard as they can, hoping to get back to shallower water and walk safely into shore. Some make it back, some become exhausted and succumb to the sea's power. The more experienced beach-goers are familiar with this potential danger and have a plan for dealing with it: don't fight the current, but swim parallel to the beach and you'll soon be free of its pull.

EN**RICH**ED

For most of your career, you've done what seems to make sense – work hard, earn as much money as you can to support your family, swim as hard as you can against the currents of life. It's a good plan, but at some point your arms grow weary from working so hard yet still not quite getting where you want to go. You can keep swimming and hope you make it – whatever 'make it' means to you. Or you can come up with a new plan that frees you from the current and takes you to a better place.

This is what the journey to a truly enriched life is. It's one where you live by a new definition of what wealth is; it's no longer about material possessions but instead it is all about escaping the tidal current of a *career* and stepping into a *life* of even deeper meaning and purpose – an abundant and fulfilled life!

That doesn't mean just leaving your job and volunteering with charities like the Red Cross. For one thing, not everyone is able to walk away from a job. And even if you could, without some careful thought and planning, you might end up trading one rip current for another. I've seen too many people get all excited about a second-half career, who jump into charitable work for which they soon lose interest, only to return to the hectic, empty and success-driven life they were trying to escape in the first place!

So how do you actually begin to make the transition to living an enriched life?

Create a business plan

It starts when you take time out to have some brainstorming sessions and then develop a plan that will take you there. The plan may be hazy at first, but in time it will become clearer and become the blueprint for the second part of your life.

What makes you tick? What do you care so deeply about, besides your family, that you'd be willing to die for? What will you be prepared to fully commit the rest of your life to?

This process of identifying what you are most passionate about may take some time. You may also benefit from interacting with others. Personally, regularly meeting with a skilled strategist who shared my values and beliefs was a critical part in helping me get greater clarity. I also found help from two great books: *Visioneering*, by Andy Stanley and *Holy Discontent*, by Bill Hybels.

When you identify that 'one thing' the next important question is, "What are you going to do about it?" You probably know from your own experience in your career that good intentions aren't enough to get the job done.

If you want to achieve results you need to develop a strategic plan and then implement it.

Over the years, I have created many business plans, so when I shifted my emphasis from purely pursuing success and the material wealth that came with that, I did what came naturally to me – I created a business plan for my second half. Only this time I built my plan around my new values. This time the focus was to align my business and career to my life-purpose, and not the other way round. In the past, I somehow hoped the other parts of my life would just miraculously fit in and around my business plan. The first part of this book is testament that this is a disaster waiting to happen!

Practical integration

Redefining wealth did not mean I quit my CEO role. But what I did do was to go about my work in a *different* way. Externally, I was still the same businessman. I stayed in the same house, drove the same car and still barracked for the same football team. But what it did mean was that I decided to focus a lot more on investing in people and helping them reach their full potential. I became more interested in relationship-building and less task-focused. My leadership style evolved to become more inclusive. I started to serve the staff and empower the management team and their staff. This meant the extra productivity of staff well and truly covered my lesser efforts as I reduced my working hours by more than twenty hours per week.

There's no magical formula about creating a business plan but in my experience, as you focus on your new dream life, I suggest your plan addresses these six components:

1 Mission

Specifically, what do you hope to actually *do*?

Just as every successful business needs a mission statement to keep it focused on what it should be doing every day, you need a mission statement to make sure you are progressively moving towards your new goal. The late Peter Drucker reportedly advised that a good mission statement ought to fit on the front of a T-shirt. In other words, it needs to be short, focused and to the point. It also needs to be measurable, pointing to specific results or outcomes you hope to achieve.

2 Money

Like it or not, doing good works requires money. How will you fund your new mission? Can you afford to quit your job and live off your investments? Can you negotiate a reduced workload agreement with your employer? Will you need to raise funds on your own? Here's where you need to be extremely clear and brutally honest about developing a budget that includes a realistic income stream.

3 Measurability

How will you know if you're accomplishing your mission? What are your KPIs (key performance indicators)? Embracing a new definition of wealth, or transitioning your effort from the desire to succeed, to wanting to do something significant, is not an excuse for mediocrity. It's motivating and inspiring to be able to see exactly how well you are doing in your new 'career,' so approach it the same way you did when you were trying to get that promotion.

4 Capacity

In terms of human resources, what do you need to get the job done? Do you plan to build your own organisation and if so, how will you recruit your team? Or are there existing organisations with similar goals that you could partner with? My one word of caution here has to do with reinventing the wheel. Why waste your time and money building an organisational infrastructure that already exists?

5 Partnership

If you are married, don't do what I did in my first half when I neglected my wife's needs and just expected her to tag along. As a fast-paced person, I needed to slow down and treat her as an equal stakeholder and partner in my new 'business plan for my parallel career.' For me, one of the great rewards of my second half journey is being able to do it with Sue. After years of being together, but with many separate priorities and focuses, it's now like being back in the days when we were first married, when we really enjoyed each other's company and had fun doing things together. I'm loving it!

All too often I see men get a fresh wind in their sails. They become excited by discovering a sense of purpose and can't wait to make significant changes. But they charge off without consulting their wives and/or other crucial stakeholders, to make sure they are on board. Big mistake! Make sure that your second half leads you on a journey that your loved ones fully support so that you can enjoy the journey together.

6 Mentorship

The sixth component to your business plan is to include one or more mentors who can help you develop your plan as well as walk alongside you on your journey. A good mentor will not only help you with your plan and provide accountability but will also help you monitor how you are doing in these five critical areas of life:

emotionally: how you are going with yourself?

relationally: how you are going with your key relationships?

spiritually: how you are going in your faith journey?

physically: how you are going with your health and fitness?

vocationally: how you are going with your career or business life?

Think of these five areas as tyres on a car (the fifth is your spare!). If any one of them gets out of shape, it can stop your journey from continuing. For me, when I was trapped on the success journey, I was like a car whose tyres were all running out of air. I was stressed out. I was becoming disconnected from Sue and my children. I had an unhealthy attitude towards God, trying to fit him into my life in a way that served me. I was plagued by constant headaches. And

I was looking for my career to satisfy the needs it was never meant to satisfy.

My point is pretty simple. It's one thing to want an enriched life – to desire to invest your life in a worthy cause – but without a specific plan, you will end up experiencing frustration. Devote as much time and creativity to this as you would a regular business plan. Enlist a few trusted friends or colleagues to review and critique your plan.

Back to the basics

Increasingly, businesses are not only paying attention to their performance in the marketplace, but are also including values and standards of integrity into their business plans. And so should you. Whether you are a person of faith or not, I suggest you consider looking to some ancient wisdom or higher purpose to guide you to think more about what values and beliefs underpin your new business plan.

When I lived only for success, the Bible often seemed mostly irrelevant to me. A dry, archaic, religious text about people whose names I couldn't pronounce. So, I turned to some great business books by people like Michael Gerber, Jim Collins, Ricardo Semler, Steven Covey and Ken Blanchard. I suspect some readers may feel the same about the Bible as I once did. Yet I still recommend it as a reliable guide for your own journey to living a new enriched life, even if you are not a religious person.

The Bible is all about a seemingly impossible dream to make the world a better place. It's the original "Big Hairy Audacious Goal" (please refer *Good to Great*). And it calls on everyone to join in that incredible task of bringing hope and healing to others. All the teaching – the wisdom and practical guidance – is aimed at showing us how to really live, rather than just exist.

The new you

It's a slogan, and probably one best saved for diet and exercise advertisements, but in the transformation to an enriched life that is full of meaning and purpose, you will feel like a different person. You'll have more energy, more imagination, more drive and more contentment than ever before!

Compared to my first half, I absolutely love going to work these days.

Not only do I get to hang out with some extraordinary and like-minded people, but I am working at my purpose every day and helping others to fulfil their goals and desires for a completely enriched life, and that is the best feeling.

Over the past ten years, since formally leaving my first half career, I have mentored and coached many business people like myself and guided them on their own journey. It's been amazing to see the impact of talented people who have changed their focus from serving themselves to becoming more 'others'-focused.

In 2010, I established a not-for-profit company called *Halftime Australia*, an organisation mirrored on Bob Buford's own organisation in Dallas, Texas. The aim was to encourage Australian business leaders and business owners to pause and get clarity on their life's mission and then help them develop an implementable plan around that. It has been especially helpful to Baby Boomers and many Gen-Xers in transitioning from focusing purely on riches and wealth, to meaning and purpose – and an enriched life. Interestingly, some Gen-Xers and Yers are from day one, aiming for a parallel career.

For me, my new career is far more exciting than my old one. Don't get me wrong. I did enjoy being a CEO of a large financial institution. But this new 'significance' career provides far more lasting 'dividends' than before. The move from my first career in Life 1 in financial planning to my Life 2 career in 'enrichment-planning' has been beyond my wildest expectations!

One day I might be meeting with the CEO of a mid-sized

company in Melbourne, helping him determine what matters most in his life. The next day I might be on a plane taking a group of executives to Northern India, where they can hardly help but rethink their own life on a much deeper basis than they could back at home. The best part about my day is that I put my head on my pillow at night and know that my time, talent and treasure is being invested in my passion and that is not just about making money, but making a difference.

" TRY NOT TO BECOME A MAN OF SUCCESS BUT A MAN OF VALUE. "

– Albert Einstein

11 Principles before performance

Any sporting enthusiast knows that you can't win the game on talent alone – it's the training done off the field that makes all the difference. Without the correct diet and fitness regime, an athlete's performance is limited. This is why most athletes have a list of habits or principles that they base their lifestyle on; wake up early, feed the body the fuel it needs and nothing it doesn't, train all day and work hard, stretch before and after training, go to bed at a reasonable hour, no caffeine or alcohol... the list goes on!

During the first half of our lives, most of us are all about performance. But to make the transition to an enriched life, we need to shift our emphasis away from performance and focus more on principles. In the same way that professional athletes live by their success principles, your new principles for living an enriched life will become the all-important foundation for building your new way of life.

ENRICH**ED**

Some years ago a friend asked, "OK, I have reached a point where I want to make my second half better than the first, but how do I go about doing that?"

"I'm glad you asked," I responded with a twinkle in my eye, and proceeded to share with him the following principles which, in my opinion, are fundamental to helping you live a life beyond your wildest dreams.

For me personally, they represent the major paradigm shifts I had to address in my thinking. Hopefully, these seven principles will help you address your own mindset and challenge your thinking as you plan towards living an enriched life.

Principle #1:
Change doesn't just happen

Success is like a drug. Even when you recognise its harmful effects, you keep looking for your next fix. I don't know how many times I said to myself, "I can't keep going like this," but I kept going. It was only when I finally admitted to myself that life wasn't going the way I wanted that I could make a commitment to change. You've probably heard the definition of insanity: doing the same thing over and over again and expecting different results. If that definition is correct, I must have been insane because I kept doing the same thing day in, day out, yet wondered why I felt so frustrated and unfulfilled.

Moving to a positive second half requires an overriding desire for change while still having unfulfilled goals and dreams. Unfulfilled desires actually can be an incredibly strong motivator.

A great example of someone who desired a radical change in the world was William Wilberforce, the son of a wealthy merchant and student at Cambridge University. In 1780, he became a member of parliament and dreamed of abolishing the slave trade in the British Empire. For eighteen years he regularly introduced anti-slavery motions in parliament but it wasn't until 1807 that the slave trade was finally abolished. In 1833, an act was passed giving freedom to all slaves in the British Empire. Wilberforce died months later in 1833.

Against overwhelming opposition William Wilberforce achieved this seemingly impossible dream. In my experience, dreams such as Wilberforce's are often powerful enough to propel people beyond any setbacks.

One of the things that kept nudging me to change in my own life was reflecting on the dreams I had as a boy. Somehow, I had lost sight of that heartfelt desire to help others and make the world a better place. But when I met the thousands of men, women and children living in poverty in Northern India, the 'fire in my belly' was rekindled and it gave me the courage to make some very big changes in my life.

Whether you are a Christian or not, I believe those dreams you had as a child were implanted in your heart by God. The Bible teaches that we are all uniquely designed for a purpose and it is only when we choose to live for that purpose that we will achieve the fulfilment we desire.

This is also commonly referred to as 'being true to oneself,' and it's easy to recognise when we aren't. Depression, a lack of motivation, mood swings, longing for a different life – all these symptoms are often indicators that something isn't quite right.

There is nothing wrong with success, but when I made a conscious choice to change my life and to redirect it towards my unfulfilled dreams, it was exhilarating.

Assignment: *If you are dissatisfied with the way or direction your life is currently going, write the following quote down and place it somewhere that you will see every day (i.e. on the bathroom mirror or near your computer screen): "I was created for a unique and special purpose. I have the power to change my life so that it reflects that purpose. I will make whatever changes are necessary to align my entire life with that purpose."*

Principle #2:
You are wired to help others

There's a reason why no matter how successful you are, it never seems to fully satisfy. That's because you were not created solely for yourself, but for others. In 2002, Rick Warren wrote a book that remained on the *New York Times* best-seller list for one of the longest periods in history and at the same time topped the *Wall Street Journal* best-seller charts: *The Purpose Driven Life*. I'm sure there are a lot of reasons for its success, but I believe the main reason it did so well is that it promised something that everyone desires: purpose – why we are here.

According to Warren, we were all created to serve others. It's in our DNA, and only when we live that out in our daily lives will we be fulfilled as human beings. This idea or notion is universal and it applies to everyone regardless of their religious inclinations, or even if they claim no religion at all. That is probably why so many people felt the urge to read the book when it was published.

When former Prime Minister of Australia, Bob Hawke, was interviewed at the age of eighty, he was asked what advice he would give to young people. He replied, "Focus on continuous learning and helping others." He's right.

Accepting that we've been created to help others is the first step; turning this conviction into positive action is the second.

However, unless we give a priority to intentionally seek out opportunities to serve others, we probably won't see the end results.

Most people would like to help others, but in today's time-poor economy there never seems to be enough time. Long working hours, text messages, urgent emails at all hours of the day and night, that Skype session at 5 o'clock in the morning – not to mention your gym membership that you're supposed to be using, and more – it often feels like you're already stretched to full capacity.

You're not alone.

But the good news is that investing in others is not only good for them, but for you too. According to author and researcher Allan Luks, after helping someone, the helper's body releases endorphins, brain chemicals that reduce pain and increase euphoria. This creates a rush of elation followed by a period of calm.

Luks' studies also suggest that volunteering and charitable giving can help ease stress and improve physical and emotional health. He lists the following positive effects of helping others:

strengthens the immune system activity

decreases the intensity and awareness of physical pain

activates positive emotions that support well-being

reduces negative attitudes that deplete well-being

enhances functions of various body systems.

(Allan Luks, *The Healing Power of Doing Good.*
iUniverse, 2001).

Assignment: *Make a list of the 'others' in your world. Make sure you include individuals, groups or organisations that could benefit from your help and that they are aligned with your interests and passions.*

If you need to jump-start your thinking, I suggest you go to www.rememberme.com.au for a list of charities in Australia. Narrow that list to three or four and then spend time learning more about their needs and how you might help them.

Principle #3:

Generosity is more than writing a cheque

I like to think I have always been generous with money. If there was a worthwhile cause, I was happy to give a sizeable donation. Also, I always contributed faithfully to the local church. But at the same time, my Dutch upbringing gave me a certain thriftiness and taught me to be careful with money.

I've since come to learn that there's a big difference between committing acts of generosity and having a *spirit* of generosity. The former is a behaviour while the latter is an attitude. My charitable giving clearly was commendable behaviour, but that didn't make me an all-round generous person. True generosity involves your whole being, not just your money – it requires your time, talent and treasure.

Many successful people invest their talent solely on their career, which provides them with financial resources (treasure) to build their little empires. They then guard what time they have jealously for themselves.

Even if they give a good amount of their money to charity, they aren't necessarily generous people. It's easy to give and to think you are generous while still living a self-focused life. A generous life is one that becomes more others-focused.

Thankfully, the opposite is also true – generosity is its own reward. The more you cultivate this spirit of giving your time, talent and treasure, the more you will gain from it.

Once you make the decision to live 24/7 with a spirit of generosity, it can change lives! In the inspirational film, *Pay It Forward* (2000), Trevor, a seventh-grader, responds to the call of his teacher to come up with a plan to change the world and act on it. Turning "pay backs" upside down, he devises "pay it forward" and seeks out three people who need some help in a "really big" way which requires some kind of sacrifice. The young boy's plan was that these three people would all understand that if they were helped, then they would also have to "pay it forward" and help three more people – thus creating a ripple effect of good will.

It's a simple idea but as this boy found out, one that took people's breathe away.

Assignment: *Watch the movie "Pay it Forward" with your whole family. Use this as a catalyst to commit a spontaneous act of generosity by giving your time, talent and treasure to a worthy cause or someone in need. Writing a cheque doesn't count. Really give from your whole being. How did you feel afterwards? How can you convert this spontaneous act into a 'spirit of generosity?'*

Principle #4:

There is no limit to your potential

Despite the downsides of success, it's pretty exciting. I don't know about you, but I always craved new challenges. I loved the adrenalin rush I got from successfully closing a deal I'd been working on for several months. Back then I just couldn't imagine selling my business early and coasting for the rest of my life. But that's what a lot of successful people do, and from what I can tell, they're either bored, miserable or both.

An enriched life isn't boring. It's actually quite the opposite.

Traditionally, people spend the first half of their adult lives climbing. They constantly work to improve their skills and gain more knowledge so that they can earn promotions and move up the ladder of success. Then, many tend to coast when they hit their middle years – usually somewhere between their forties and fifties. If they're wealthy enough, they often trade their full-on lives for the golf course or the cruise ship. It doesn't take long before they become caricatures of the very people they used to make fun of!

Others become worn out, tired and simply weary from years on the treadmill of life.

That's what makes discovering your life purpose so appealing. It allows you to keep climbing, but on your own terms and towards your own goals that bring more meaning and purpose to your life. My new career lets me experience that same adrenalin rush I got from growing my business but with the added satisfaction that my business makes life better for others who otherwise might not have had a chance to succeed.

As long as you keep climbing, there is no limit to what you can achieve in your new career.

Assignment: *Compile a 'bucket list' of all the things you would like to accomplish before you die – hopefully this will include some legacy items and your personal ideas. Then pick one of those 'impossible dreams' and write down the steps it would take to turn that dream into reality. Set a date and take the first step.*

Principle #5:

Retirement is not an option

There are many great examples of people who have refused to simply slip into a comfortable early retirement. One of the most inspiring men I've ever met, was the late Melbourne philanthropist, Eugene Veith, or 'Curly,' as he preferred to be known. According to Curly, the word 'retirement' was not in his vocabulary and until he died at the age of ninety-five, this old ex-truckie was busy giving most of his money away. His motto, was "I live simply so others may simply live." In 1974, at age fifty-eight, he sold his business, *Veith Transport*, then spent the next four decades giving away in excess of $20 million through his not-for-profit organisation, *Mission Enterprises*.

Likewise, Peter Drucker, the "father of modern management," continued working until his death at age ninety-five. He wrote more books after he was sixty-five years old than before.

These remarkable men knew what many gerontologists are only recently discovering – that meaningful work not only adds life to your years, but years to your life.

The reality is that when men turn fifty, they will most likely have at least another twenty-five healthy, energetic and productive years ahead of them (women will have slightly more). That's enough time for an entirely new career! So why spend it in a rocking chair?

In fact, your most productive years could be in your sixties and seventies. Just look at a few of these 'older' people who have made tremendous contributions to society in their twilight years:

Peter Mark Roget, a distinguished British scientist, was forced to retire at age seventy, so began working on a project to scientifically order language. The book was published when he was seventy-three. We know it as *Roget's Thesaurus*.

Mahatma Gandhi was sixty-one when he led the famous "Salt March," which was credited as the central moment in the fight for India's independence from England.

Corazon 'Cory' Aquino was a soft-spoken housewife in her fifties when she became the leader of a popular movement that overthrew Filipino dictator Ferdinand Marcos. She later became the first female president of the Philippines.

Why retire and risk missing the best, most productive and exciting years of your life?

Assignment: *Using an internet search engine such as Google, type in the words "never retire" and spend some time reading the articles that appear. Then select a friend or family member who has officially retired and invite him or her to lunch. Ask the following questions: "What is retirement like for you? Is it delivering the benefits you thought it would? If you had your time over again, what would you do differently? And finally, "I'm considering a different kind of retirement where I continue working but on something that I'm passionate about – what's your advice?*

Principle # 6:

There's no perfect plan or perfect moment

People often ask me when they should jump into a second-half career or a career that is based on meaning and purpose. I always urge them to be just as 'reckless' and impulsive as they were when they were younger. You remember those days, don't you? You jumped at the next opportunity even though you didn't have all the answers or a plan that guaranteed success. I don't know about you, but I often 'winged' my way through a lot of projects because I knew I could make it up as I went along, and confidently felt I would eventually get the job done.

Too many people become more cautious and conservative as they get older, avoiding risk at all cost. I know of a few mates who love the idea of a much more enriched second half but who have spent five years working on the perfect plan and waiting for the perfect moment. If you wait for the perfect moment, you'll never get there because the perfect moment doesn't exist.

Reclaim that spirit of adventure that defined you in your earlier years. Approach this new career with the same energy and fearlessness that fuelled your ambition when you were twenty and all you had was half a chance. It can be messy at first. It's like any start-up – you may have to figure it out on the run and make changes as you go. What's wrong with that?

Although I didn't wait for the perfect time, I did wait for the right time. There is a profound difference between the two. The right time to start may seem far from perfect. For me, when I had God's peace and a strong sense that now is the moment to act, I jumped in with confidence.

Assignment: *Take a long weekend getaway with your spouse, friend, or by yourself but don't make any plans. Just get in your car and take off. Decide where you'll go after you leave your house. Where will you stay? Figure it out on the way. You'll think of something. What will you do when you get there? Whatever looks like fun. After you get back, compare this getaway with a previous one where you planned every detail. Was this spontaneous trip significantly worse than the planned one? Or was it better? What might happen if you began your second half journey or parallel career the same way?*

Principle #7:
Accountability is your friend

Most wealthy people acknowledge that they are not completely responsible for their own success. They had a great team of people to help them, or they might have had a special mentor, partner or an advisory board they could turn to for advice and encouragement. If you want to be successful in your second-half career, I suggest you recruit a few trusted individuals with whom you can be completely vulnerable and transparent. These should be people who have already travelled the same journey and are willing to sacrifice their agenda to spend time speaking into your dreams, plans and aspirations.

Throughout my career I've always tried to find people who brought expertise and knowledge on board that I didn't have, and then I did my best to learn from them. These people made me a better CEO, but only because I was willing to listen to them – even when they told me things I didn't want to hear. Today, such people still make me more effective in living an enriched life.

The temptation in the second half is to believe you've finally arrived and don't need any help as you embark on this new venture. Big mistake. You're going to face new challenges and overcome unfamiliar barriers, and if you go at it alone you'll likely find out you're not cut out for a parallel career and head right back to the rat race.

In all that I have done throughout my career – whether it was building Garrisons, helping with the school or the church, working in India with Jossy or starting up Halftime Australia – I always did it by looking for one unique individual with the same values and purpose and for whom I had the utmost respect. It had to be someone I could closely team up with to achieve the vision and, in my case, this usually meant we ended up working as partners.

I work best when someone else's strengths are able to cover my weaknesses. This way, we could team up together to achieve the goal or the vision.

I like to share openly and be transparent with my business partners and those who are part of my team. I regularly ask them for feedback. This helps keep me accountable. It also provides encouragement through a few words of wisdom and sometimes offers affirmation or clarity that I am on the right path. Unfortunately, a lot of people fear accountability because they think it means getting caught doing something wrong. Accountability is ninety per cent encouragement – a comforting voice affirming what you are doing and offering ideas to help you do it better.

If you are married or in a long-term relationship, I strongly recommend you include your partner wherever possible in your second half journey. After all, the changes you make in your life will affect your spouse as well, and if he/she is fully on board you will both benefit.

Assignment: *Make a list of six people in your life whom you trust and admire. Beside each name, write down two or three qualities or skill-sets they have that appeal to you. Go over that list to select two or three people you would most like to have as your mentor and cheerleader. Then, meet with each of these individuals and share your vision for making the transition from success to an enriched life and ask them if they will serve on your team going forward.*

There's nothing magical about these seven principles but they worked for me. They served as a checklist to keep me focused on my goal.

If you begin with these principles and make them the foundation of your plan, they will help provide a great framework to pursue your life's mission.

" WITH GREAT POWER COMES GREAT RESPONSIBILITY. "

– Spiderman

12 Moral compass

One of the problems associated with success is that people will sometimes do anything to achieve it. It's that 'win at all cost' mentality that can insidiously creep into our lives as we justify ethical shortcuts as part of the 'cost' of doing business. By its very nature, living an enriched life demands the highest moral and ethical standards.

You can't have much of a legacy if you're always looking over your shoulder.

Throughout your journey, your character will be tested because you have taken a stand for the greater good. A well-known friend of mine, and one of our clients at Halftime Australia, Kevin Bailey, is the perfect illustration of how this happens. Kevin reached a point in his life and career where he was searching for ways to be more significant – he was already a successful public figure both in Melbourne and internationally, but during the

Indonesian occupation of East Timor in 1991, there was a terrible massacre of over 200 teenage students and Kevin felt convicted to help the oppressed people of East Timor in some way.

He contacted Abel Guterres, the spokesperson for the East Timorese community in Melbourne, offering his services and was quickly told the best course of action would be to join in a protest march along the streets of Melbourne and be part of a rally outside the Indonesian Consulate the next day. This wasn't the type of 'help' Kevin had anticipated. He was a public figure in the finance world and a well-known author and radio and TV show presenter. It wouldn't be the best thing for his reputation to be seen holding a placard like some unionist on a picket line or tree-hugging hippie. Besides, he had a job to go to. But after careful consideration, he decided to join the protest. The next day, and many times over the next decade, Kevin continued to agitate for social justice and the right of self-determination for the oppressed Timorese in any way he could.

When at last the Timorese were given the chance to vote for self-determination, Kevin took leave to go to East Timor in 1999 and help with the task of rebuilding the fledgling nation out of the ashes of the destruction of the vengeful departing military. Over the course of the next few years and many subsequent visits, he became close to the new president, prime minister and leadership of the emerging nation who asked him to establish a consulate in Australia to help represent them and strengthen links between the two countries. He also shared his investment skills with the government and became involved in many church and non-profit organisations, helping ordinary people rebuild their lives after years of war.

It wasn't easy for Kevin to get involved, but he did it because it was right – he simply could not ignore injustice even if it meant standing in the bitter Melbourne cold holding a "Free East Timor" sign.

Left field challenge

Shortly after I wrote down the thirteen things that had to change in my life, my own commitment to integrity was challenged in a huge and very uncomfortable manner. It was about two years after my company, Garrisons, had been sold to *Challenger*, part of the Packer Group. I woke up one morning to reports on radio, television and in the newspaper that a number of legal firms in Hobart which had solicitors first mortgage funds were about to collapse.

My head started to hurt. Garrisons had over $2 million from thirty clients invested in these funds. These clients were predominantly retirees looking to stretch out their superannuation. We'd placed the investments a couple of years earlier while I was the major shareholder and held the top job. A few of our advisers had recommended clients to invest in the solicitors first mortgage funds and now their money was gone. I suppose I could have just blamed the advisers and forgotten about it, but if you look back at my list, at least five of the commitments had to do with integrity. One that sort of jumped out at me as I thought about those investors was 'Be prepared to make a fool of myself in pursuing what I know is right'.

But I knew it wouldn't be easy.

Under the microscope

A former union official who'd represented workers on Tasmania's hydro-electricity scheme was one of the clients who had lost money from the collapse of these investments. Aged in his sixties at the time, Bob (not his real name) was an imposing figure with striking silver hair, firm facial features, and a stance that suggested he was ready for a fight.

With decades of union experience, he was highly skilled at orchestrating campaigns highlighting injustice, and we'd lost his money. Once it became apparent that this was going to take years to sort out, he didn't waste any time rallying disgruntled investors to march on the offices of the *Tasmanian Law Society*, the offices of solicitors involved in the fund, and of course our offices at Garrisons. His aim was to attract media attention and to make life uncomfortable for everyone who'd had a hand in losing the money. And his plan was working. With megaphone in hand, he whipped the outraged mob into a flag-waving, saucepan-beating frenzy. Once a week, his posse arrived outside our Hobart offices on the main street for a two-hour protest that was carefully timed to catch the attention of peak-hour traffic. They made so much noise that a television crew from *A Current Affair* flew down from Victoria for the story and accosted our financial controller, Michael Spinks, in the stairwell to demand explanations on camera. Things went from bad to worse when the *Australian Securities & Investments Commission* (ASIC) began questioning research we'd done to safeguard our investors. At the same time the Federal Labor Government saw the circus as an ideal time to hold a senate inquiry in Hobart into investor protection. So Garrisons' financial controller, compliance officer, two financial advisers, and I were called before the inquiry to give evidence in what became a very public witch-hunt.

Meanwhile, the protests continued. Angry investors indiscriminately targeted anyone connected with the business, from receptionists to managers. It devastated me to see our team of hard-working staff become targets for abuse. Staff had worked for years to build and uphold the company's reputation for integrity and in a matter of weeks it was in tatters. Morale took a severe beating. Sick days increased.

An integrity test I didn't welcome

I could hardly blame our disgruntled investors for turning militant; some had lost their entire savings. If I were in that situation I'd probably head for the saucepan cupboard too.

The bad publicity was taking its toll on Garrisons' client base, even clients whose investments had nothing to do with solicitors first mortgages. My dream was starting to unravel. More than a decade of work at building a brand with a great reputation was quickly disintegrating. But for me it was bigger than what was happening to the company. I began to realise that this was an integrity test for me.

I had to do something.

I met with Bob at our offices and assured him that we were doing everything we could to recover the investments, but he wasn't convinced and stepped-up the saucepan beating campaign. Over the next few weeks I met with various Tasmanian government officials and when that didn't produce results I flew to Canberra to seek intervention from federal politicians, but at every turn I was stonewalled.

For the record, I had already received a payout for my share in the business so there was no personal financial gain for recouping the clients' investments. I was driven by an obligation to our clients, staff and to securing the long-term future of the business. I was proud of the company's dedication to integrity and knew I couldn't continue as its leader unless I led it out of the present mess. I thought back to when I was a boy and the Tasmanian Governor Lord Rowallan's letter, and how he went to the trouble of making sure I received my shilling. It was only a shilling, but I remember how grateful I was that someone had looked out for me. I couldn't imagine what our investors were going through, having lost $2 million and waiting hopelessly, although noisily, for someone to look out for them.

Drawing a line in the sand

I flew to Sydney and rolled out a two-hour presentation to the management at Challenger. I'd never spoken with more passion. I tried to convince them to take over the investments from our clients and reimburse them 100 per cent, and then for Challenger to pursue the Law Society and legal firms for reimbursement. The company had a better chance of success than the clients, I argued. I closed the presentation by encouraging them to consider the $2 million reimbursement as an insurance premium to protect Garrisons, which was now worth close to $100 million, but its value was being eroded daily!

I couldn't have been happier with my presentation and was extremely confident that the chief executive would reach for the cheque book. But after deliberating for a few hours, management said "no." I left the room in shock, but quickly returned and threatened to resign if they didn't give me a cheque for $2 million to take back to our clients. They shrugged and still said "no."

That's when I decided to live out that new commitment of doing something foolish for a greater good.

I returned to the meeting room one last time and declared, "I plan to stay here until you give me the money for my clients!" I then calmly took a seat in the waiting area and spent the rest of the day reading magazines and chatting with the receptionist. At the end of the day I went back to my hotel, only to return promptly at 9:00 a.m. the next day. And the next. And the next.

I'll admit it seemed rather foolish for the CEO of a major company to engage in a 'sit-in' like some disgruntled student. People coming and going must have wondered what that guy in the suit was doing sitting in the waiting area all day, but when you're committed to a mission, you do extraordinary things.

And it worked. Well, sort of.

After several days one of the directors called me into his office to say they'd changed their minds. They would reimburse our investors!

Embracing the enemy

I was a happy man flying back to Hobart with the problem behind me.

However, when I met Bob to tell him the good news he wasn't so euphoric. He was enjoying his role as a media celebrity, he seemed a whole foot taller, and said reimbursement alone wasn't good enough. He was demanding interest on top of the principal. So, I again ended up at Challenger's offices, this time asking for another $300,000. After more wrangling, they eventually agreed and within weeks we'd repaid our investors. The clients were extremely grateful and despite the trauma, most of them amazingly decided to keep their investments with Garrisons.

I arranged another meeting with Bob, who eased out of his militant stance after being reimbursed, and shocked him by offering him a job as a consultant to help the company recoup money from the Tasmanian Law Society. *The Mercury*, Tasmania's largest newspaper, ran a page-three story with a large photograph of Bob and I joining forces. People couldn't believe I had embraced the enemy. He went from being our biggest opponent to our biggest proponent and reversed the bad publicity with comments to the media about how the company had acted with integrity to support its clients.

Values for a purpose driven life?

It's relatively easy to make a list of things you hope will guide you into a life of greater purpose, but actually living up to those commitments is not so easy. Especially when things don't go as well as you hoped. For me, I had to decide whether I would walk the talk. I had to decide whether to fight for those who had been disadvantaged as a result of advice received by my company, or to wipe my hands and say that it really wasn't my problem.

The true test of your character will not come in the heady moments of planning and dreaming about your new life of purpose. It's when you begin to live out that dream that you will be tempted to make an exception 'just this once' for the greater good of your mission. But if you hold true to those values that once seemed so noble, you will enjoy that reckless abandonment to integrity that allows you to do something others might call foolish – something that history calls courageous.

"   SUCCESS IS WHAT WE DO FOR OURSELVES; SIGNIFICANCE IS WHAT WE DO FOR OTHERS.   "

– John Maxwell

13 Second half options

When my kids were young, they loved nothing more than hooning around the quiet streets by our seaside holiday house, riding their bicycles. It gave them the freedom they longed for, and if I'm honest, gave me the peace and quiet I needed to unwind. Like most kids, they each had a different sized bike for their heights and abilities. My eldest, Alice, had the biggest – a women's five-speed bicycle that she and Sue shared. It was a gentle ride and suited them both perfectly. My son, Heath, had a rusty old BMX that he liked to thrash about with and do tricks on. Renee had a middle-range, hand-me-down bike from her older sister and little Jess was still on her training wheels. Each had a bike that best suited their abilities and requirements.

The right 'bike' or mode of transport to take you on your journey to significance will depend on your own ability and situation. It will depend on what path you want to take. Not everyone is able to quit their day job, which raises an important question: do you need to drop everything and spend all your time on a career focused on enriching the lives of others?

In a word, no. We can't all jump hell-for-leather onto a BMX-styled second career; some of us will require a gentler ride. In the same way you would invest time into researching the best bike for a long-distance marathon race, you will need to pick the best option or 'mode of transport' to get you on the right path.

This was good news for me because I wanted to keep my hand in business and stay connected to the energy and vitality of the commercial world.

Finding the right option for you

Over the years of meeting and mentoring many Halftimers like myself, I've found there are a variety of different strategies that can be used to launch your second career. These might include the following options.

Low-cost probe

In Texas when the oil industry wants to investigate whether oil is likely to be present, they will often look for an inexpensive method which requires little effort or commitment. They call this a low-cost probe. It's a way of gently putting your foot in the water.

I took a low-cost probe when I went to India with Jossy for the first time. I hadn't abandoned my career; I hadn't made a long-term commitment. I hadn't made a huge investment. It took only a limited amount of time. In effect, it was a 'taste and see'. Of course, I was hooked from that moment on, but others will try a low-cost probe and conclude 'that's not for me' and back out or change direction relatively easily.

Parallel career

A parallel career is one that occurs at the same time as you are pursuing your current career. While I was still CEO at Garrisons, I took on leadership and board responsibilities with the school and the church.

My business partner, Tim O'Neill, similarly decided to follow a parallel career during an horrific year when seven people that he and his wife knew committed suicide. After seeing a real need in their community of Launceston, their hearts were moved to start a local church that could provide hope and support for people who were desperate for answers in their lives. It could have been risky for Tim to leave the business world and step into the unknown. Instead he played safe by opting for a parallel career for five years. Today, *The Tailrace Centre* is a hub for the community and includes a vibrant community Church, a business centre, conference facilities, wedding chapel, reception facility, café, restaurant and amazing kids' play centre.

Second career

As the name suggests, this type of option is for people who want to have a completely new second career. It might be something completely different to your first vocation, or it may not. I'm in my second career now. I'm still using the same skills as in my first career, but I'm using them in addition to new skills I have developed.

David Clark is a good friend of mine who is also in his second career. Previously, he was a successful financial planner and corporate executive. Today, David uses his skills and experience to help people find their 'fit' in the workforce, their business and in personal relationships. The best bit is he gets a real kick out of helping people find their life-purpose. Admittedly, David had to adjust his lifestyle accordingly. He downsized in every area so he could live on a third of his previous income, yet he's never been happier or more fulfilled.

Portable career

In these days of modern communications and high-speed travel, it's possible for knowledge workers to live on one side of the world and bring their skills to those living in a completely different hemisphere. Think big and think global! One mentor who works with me regularly coaches clients from interstate and overseas using travel, telephone and Skype.

Where could your skills be best used? Perhaps it's in your local community, or maybe it's somewhere you have never even physically been before? Don't be limited by location.

Business realignment

Business realignment provides an opportunity for business owners to pursue their life-purpose through their businesses. This can happen when your life mission is reflected in the vision of your business. By staying with your existing organisation you are able to utilise the people and resources you already have, rather than starting afresh. It's a great option to consider.

This is exactly what three Halftime clients of mine have done. John De Bruyn, his brother and cousin, have a successful major trucking and transport business. In pursuing significance they decided to stay in their family business rather than sell it. They were motivated to embark on an aggressive growth strategy so they could use the growing profits to provide funding for numerous important local community and third-world philanthropic projects. They realigned the vision of their business to their passions and life mission and are having the time of their lives helping others.

It's really about focus

The question still remains: is it possible to engage in a new second-half career if you aren't well off enough to quit your job and live off your investments? What if you enjoy your career and don't want to leave it but still feel the need for meaning in your life?

The best way to answer that is to remind you that it is not about your job or the amount of money you have amassed, but it's about your focus. You redefine the meaning of wealth when you shift your attention from yourself to helping others.

One of the reasons you may be feeling unfulfilled in your current work could be that your focus has shifted. For most of us, this happens slowly over time. You spend most of your energy advancing your career and growing your net worth and there's no time left over for others. As I've said earlier, this is not necessarily a conscious decision to be selfish. It's a by-product of a success-driven lifestyle. Of course, in an ideal world we might fantasise about quitting our job and helping the poor, but the reality is that this type of fantasy isn't possible for most of us.

In the real world, if everyone quit their job to help those less fortunate they would have very short second-half careers. Regardless of your good intentions, you still have to feed your family and pay your bills. Fortunately you do have options.

Money is important too

When this issue comes up with people considering the transition from pure success to one full of meaning and purpose, I ask them to calculate their current regular living expenses – how much money they need annually to maintain their lifestyle. Then I ask a little tougher question: how much, if any, are you willing to cut back on that amount? Whatever number they eventually come up with becomes the minimum amount of income they need to be able to generate from either their investments or some form of employment.

The next money question has to do with the nature of your second-half career. What exactly will you be doing and what additional expenses will this incur? For example, do you plan to launch your own charitable organisation? If so, there will be considerable expenses. Even if you partner with existing organisations, you may have to cover incidental expenses and hire an executive assistant to handle the administration work.

My final money question is, how will you cover the costs of your second-half career? Will you have enough income from your investments to cover these costs? Will you try to raise funds through donations? Will you charge for your services? Will you need to continue working at your current job? Or will it be a combination of all of these? Perhaps you will be able to structure a business that enables you to receive the income that you need while pursuing your purpose and utilising the people and resources of your business?

Once you determine your personal budget as well as a budget for your second-half enterprise it may become clear you cannot afford to quit your job. If so, here is an example of how a successful businessman got around the funding problem by tapping into government funding.

Many companies have recognised the value of giving back to their communities by providing opportunities and incentives for their employees to volunteer. For example, the *Australian Business and Community Network* (ABCN) sponsors a variety of programs for businesses to support economically disadvantaged schools. One of their programs pairs executives with school principals to share leadership goals and challenges. In 2007, Minter Ellison finance partner, John Poulsen, was paired with WA's Wambro Community High School principal, Sydney Parke, to identify and groom leaders from the economically disadvantaged school. The school benefitted from Poulsen's leadership acumen, and he gained the satisfaction that comes from helping others while still continuing in his job. (WA Business News, 1 March 2007)

Significance in smaller doses

Initially, the Halftime movement appealed primarily to men in their fifties who had logged twenty to twenty-five years in their careers. This is especially true for people in my Baby-Boomer generation. But I've since learned that Generations X and Y are a little more impatient and want their lives to count much sooner. For them, or for anyone who may not have other options, I recommend using annual leave time and weekends to engage in any number of 'other-directed' volunteer activities. Australia ranks number one among developed nations in the number of paid days off for workers with a minimum of ten years tenure: thirty-one days, including national holidays. That could mean up to thirty-one days annually of you enriching many people's lives, including your own! This is a great way to find what you are most passionate about and prepare for a greater commitment when the opportunity arises.

You will encounter speed humps

It would be easy to assume we could slide seamlessly into pursuing an enriched life without encountering too many difficulties. After all, many of us have decades of work experience under our belts. Some of us have been at the top of our game and proven ourselves in sales and management. We have a reputation for being a respectable business leader. Maybe you've even won an award or two.

For me, this mindset was the first speed hump I had to overcome. I didn't realise how dependent I was on the people around me. In the past, if I required marketing help I'd call in the smart, young marketing manager and she would consult with her team and deliver whatever I needed. Likewise, I had a highly competent executive assistant at my beck and call. I had a workshop presenter, an IT department – you know what I'm talking about.

In my exuberance to follow my new career, I had given insufficient consideration to the fact that my skill level was high in a very narrow area and my competency outside of that was way below average. I was shocked to find that the not-for-profit areas I stepped into simply lacked the resources or cash flow to fund the basic infrastructure support I was accustomed to. While there were many passionate volunteers, invariably they lacked required specialist skills and were usually part-time and overloaded with too much work.

Let's look at an example from the sporting world. Recently, several AFL club teams decided to entice top-line well-known rugby league players to switch codes from rugby to Australian Rules football – the idea was that this would help boost interest from Sydney fans over to AFL. The Sydney rugby players were offered mega bucks to switch sports, with management naively believing that one type of football (NRL) required pretty similar skill-sets to the other (AFL). While this experiment is still in its early days, experts are now saying that despite these players being exceptional rugby players, they may only ever become average players in Australian Rules football – even after three years of intense learning and undertaking lots of extra skills training. Hopefully the critics will be proven wrong, but this is common in other sports such as baseball. Just because someone is a great pitcher, doesn't mean he can score runs. The skill-sets are different, despite both athletes being great baseball players.

This is a similar problem facing many Baby Boomers. They think that being successful in business means they have the skill-sets to make it in any venture they put their hands to. But on the journey to a career dedicated to enriching the lives of others, you might find you simply lack the right skills. It's no different than when you started your first career. Maybe you went to university or underwent a traineeship or night-school course; perhaps you volunteered in an area where you needed some practical experience. It makes sense that when you shift your focus to a new second half career you will need some other skills to add to your repertoire.

When I moved into my second career, I hired a public speaking coach because I knew I needed to improve in this area. It wasn't fun. She grilled me, poked fun at my presentation skills, and pushed me to my limits. But without that training, I would never have had the confidence and ability to speak to groups of business leaders and inspire them to live a better second-half.

What skills would help you in your second half?

What do I put on my business card?

Loss of identity is another speed hump for many high-flying successful leaders. As they try to transition from a successful business career into the not-for-profit sector they often feel naked without their big, corporate title. This is understandable when you have spent years being labelled as the head of a company or someone with a prestigious title on your business card.

One heartfelt statement that keeps coming up as I work with entrepreneurs and business leaders could be summarised by this gentleman's remarks: "I have been the CEO for fifteen years and in charge of the vision and made all the key decisions. Plus I have had a large workforce at my disposal and a big budget. Everyone deferred to me. In fact, everyone looked to me as the leader. But now I don't have a proper position or a whole raft of people ready to respond to my every need or to my every directive. To be honest I am lost without being able to put CEO on my business card."

Another high-level leader put it this way: "I am a leader but I have no followers and I feel lost!"

My wife often felt frustrated when people asked her, "What exactly does your husband do these days?" The question was difficult because there wasn't a clear answer, and for a while you might find yourself in the same boat. During the transitional stage of forming a new identity in your second half, things can look a bit messy for a while, but that's okay. In fact, that's part of the fun. If you need a title, give yourself one! Why not put 'adventurer' or 'chief excitement officer' on a business card and enjoy the look of envy from your old mates when you hand one to them!

The great thing about trading your old view of success for a new definition of wealth is that there's no 'right way' to do it. You're finally freed from the rules and bureaucracy that chained you to your desk for all those years. Depending on your current circumstances, you can create and execute a plan that will allow you to focus some or all of your time, talent and treasure on others. And as your career and financial position changes, you can adapt your plan accordingly.

In other words, you can always trade that comfortable road bike for a BMX as the terrain of your second-half career changes. Either way, it's still a fun ride.

" LIFE IS A DARING ADVENTURE OR IT IS NOTHING AT ALL. "

– Helen Keller

14 No risk, no reward

Australian thrill-seeker, A. J. Hackett, introduced bungee jumping to the world by illegally jumping off the Eiffel Tower in 1987. He has since created something of a bungee-jumping empire with facilities in Australia, New Zealand, France, Germany, Russia and Macau. People from all walks of life – ranging in ages from ten to eighty – travel to these sites for the sole purpose of jumping off a high tower with nothing but a strong rubber band keeping them from plunging to their deaths.

Why?

According to one of Hackett's associates, "People jump to achieve the adrenalin rush that comes from pushing yourself past your fear."

I've never bungee jumped, nor do I plan to anytime soon. But I get it. I understand why people seek thrills in bungee jumping and other extreme sports where failure could mean serious injury or death.

High risk brings high rewards.

Risk is part of normal everyday life whether it's driving a car, crossing a road or flying in a plane. Most of us take risks without even thinking about it. But for many successful people the issue of taking on new risk and the fear of failure can be daunting, especially as we get older.

One of the biggest battles I face with clients I coach is their attitude towards taking risks. The reason they shy away from the unknown can vary but most commonly it's due to the fact that they took big risks only early on in their careers. Then, as they became more successful and took on both family and financial responsibilities, their attachment to their level of lifestyle and the predictability of their career basically paralysed them. On the one hand, they want their second half to really count, but at the same time, they cannot shift their mindset away from the treadmill of success and the fear of failure. *What if I lose heaps of my money? What if I look stupid? What if this venture doesn't work, what will people think?*

Over the years, I have come to see that people who make things happen are always risk-takers. But often when we have accumulated enough assets to be comfortable, we think we should enjoy our success and don't want to risk losing it. And so we trade off some of our original DNA and move from being a risk-taker to a caretaker. But the problem is that if we aren't risking, we won't grow, and when we don't grow, we will inevitably decline. So in this way, we move from being a caretaker to an undertaker. And a part of us dies with it.

There's a long list of negative outcomes that we can easily worry about, but what many people lose sight of is what could happen if they succeed.

Famous nineteenth century inventor and entrepreneur, Thomas Edison, freely admitted that the majority of his experiments didn't succeed. But rather than worrying that he would never have a breakthrough, Edison kept plugging away. He eventually succeeded in inventing the first telephone, the light bulb, the phonograph and the first motion picture camera. In fact, he became the fourth most prolific inventor in history holding 1,093 patents and he did all this despite being deaf in one ear and eighty per cent deaf in the other!

Why taking risks can be worth it

For some, the idea of failing might not be overwhelming, but I've found many successful business men and women have lost sight of the reward that taking big risks can bring despite being 'vision-builders'. They prefer to make 'safe' decisions and have back-up plans. Please understand, I am not suggesting these things are bad. In fact, they are responsible and mature mind-sets that we develop throughout our lives and careers. Being risk-averse is considered good business practice. However, playing it too safe can seriously undermine the possibility for a truly worthwhile second-half career.

Recently, I learned of an inspiring young gentleman who took a big risk that paid massive dividends – not just financially, but it changed the way he and others viewed the world.

In 2012, the television show *American Idol* introduced the world to Scott MacIntyre, a blind young man with a captivating voice that won the heart of a nation. As a little blind boy, Scott probably never considered that one day he would enter a competition like *American Idol*, let alone overcome all the obstacles stacked against him to give the energetic, choreographed performance that he did.

So, how did Scott MacIntyre conquer his disability and find the nerve to risk humiliating himself on live television? It wasn't just an impulsive decision – it was due to a habit he had developed and nurtured over time, starting from when he was very young.

Every year when he was a small child, Scott's family would take a road trip to a rustic getaway called Trinity Alps Resort, in northern California. They stayed in old wooden cabins, grilled freshly-caught fish and swam in a swimming hole along the river. It was a great holiday retreat and Scott cherished spending time outdoors but he was also acutely aware that there were some things he wasn't able to do. In particular, there was a foot-bridge that stretched above the swimming hole nearby. The older children would jump off it into the water below. But the jump had to be executed precisely, as there was only one spot that was deep enough. One summer, Scott was determined to try the jump despite his blindness. He wasn't completely comfortable with the idea at first as he had heard the other kids scream as they jumped from high above. But Scott also knew that when the jump was over, those kids came up out of the water laughing and having a great time. Determined to have a go, Scott asked his dad if he would do the jump with him. He agreed. As Scott and his father walked out onto the bridge they could faintly hear the muffled sounds of people swimming below but there was no way for Scott to see how high up they were; all he could do was step off the bridge, trusting that he would land in the water and not on a rock. His dad counted to three, and they jumped together. The feeling of free-falling through the air was incredible and as soon as they surfaced and caught their breath, little Scott asked his dad if they could do it again!

Bigger risk, bigger reward

Taking that jump was risky. But even at a young age, Scott MacIntyre realised the reward was high enough to take the plunge. It was with this same mindset that Scott released his first CD at eleven years old. It also gave him the confidence to live in London on his own, and years later Scott had the courage to audition as the first-ever blind contestant on *American Idol*. He had to wonder though – would he have even chosen to audition if he hadn't decided to jump off the bridge in Trinity Alps?

People who achieve their dreams are people who are not afraid to take risks. In the end, we all have a choice: to let fear of what might happen keep us from reaching our goals and dreams, or to take a leap of faith into the unknown and learn as we go.

I've never jumped off a high bridge or, as I said before, bungee jumped, but after my own life-changing trip to Northern India in 2003, I finally felt ready to take the plunge and jump feet first into my new career. Within a few days of returning home from New Delhi, Jossy called saying he wanted to meet. By this stage we had become close acquaintances, if not good friends, and I respected and admired the work he did immensely.

My leap of faith

We had barely got past the opening pleasantries when Jossy boldly delivered the following offer: "John, how would you like to join the board of *Empart* and become my chairman?" It was a double-edged offer. It offered all the things I craved - importantly, helping others and using my gifts for a purpose greater than myself. But it didn't offer security or success.

I felt a similar feeling as Scott MacIntyre must have encountered jumping off that bridge. I felt a little apprehensive about the risks involved but at the same time, determined to achieve the reward I felt was waiting for me in my second-half career.

I wasn't wearing rose-coloured glasses. I knew there were potential risks involved in Jossy's offer. The change in career meant Sue and I would have to sell our dream home and holiday beach shack to move interstate from Hobart to Melbourne. We would have to leave behind all our friends and family and there was no offer of a salary on the table. It would be like starting out all over again. Yet, amazingly, this move came at a perfect time for us. I had already sold the company and recruited a CEO to replace me, plus all the children had moved out of home.

"Jossy, my friend," I replied. "Nothing would give me more pleasure, but let me first talk it over with Sue..."

Thankfully, Sue was extremely encouraging about the move and it was with her full love and support that we left behind our comfortable lifestyle to start again in Melbourne.

The first thing Sue did ahead of our move was coax me into buying a big rundown house on a large property in Warrandyte, a quaint old gold mining town just thirty minutes' drive from the city, and close to Jossy's office. It might have been 'quaint' but it definitely wasn't my first choice of accommodation. The house itself was a far cry from the nice luxuries I had taken for granted. There was no garage, the interior was tired and the so-called tennis court was really overgrown and neglected with a broken net sagging to one side. However, the house had the potential to suit our needs and it was reasonably priced. Over the next few years, Sue devoted her time and energy into supporting me and totally renovating our home. As it turned out, this was the biggest blessing I could ask for. During those years, this large house became the overnight accommodation for our interstate children and their families, also international and interstate guests.

When you start to think big the types of people who fall into your life and your home is incredible! I can truly say that my second-half has enriched not only my own life but also the life of my wife and family, often in ways I had never contemplated or dreamed of. It's quite ironic – as I invest my life into others and their success, I have been incredibly blessed. And guess what? No headaches!

On moving to Melbourne, my second-half career plan was relatively straight forward. Firstly, I was leaving behind my old career in financial planning for good! I was now in the position that I could dedicate most of my time and energy into doing work which helped others succeed. Next on my plan was joining up with Jossy as the board chairman of *Empart*. Then, I set up my own boutique coaching company. The sole purpose for doing this was to mentor business people like myself who needed help transitioning from a successful career into a more meaningly and purposeful second career.

For the first time in my life I was completely satisfied with my lot and it had nothing to do with my bank balance. My 'success' wasn't measured by numbers or large wealthy clients but on something much deeper. Every day I had the opportunity to sow into someone's life and make a massive difference and it felt fantastic. Suddenly, by changing my career and focus, I felt like the richest man in the world. That doesn't mean it was painless or easy all of the time. There were many challenges along the way, but the satisfaction I felt on a day-to-day basis was strong enough to keep me focused and on track.

One problem with life balance

In the late 1980s and early '90s, a whole new industry developed around the notion of wellness and life balance. It became so popular and permeating that even the corporate sector began to embrace this as a means to improve morale and productivity in organisations. Generally, this had been a very positive thing because the issues it addressed, such as the lack of exercise, poor diet and workaholism, are important imbalances that needed to be addressed, at home and at work.

However, I have one problem with life balance. Jim Collins, in his book, *Good to Great*, made a valid and good point about how "Good is the enemy of Great" and if we are satisfied with something being *good* we can easily become complacent and fail to go beyond that to achieve greatness.

Many business people I have met struggle with the concept of changing from success and wealth to an enriched life, especially when they realise that it often requires sacrifice and discomfort on their part to benefit others. The idea of 'work-life balance' is often a stumbling block that stops people from ever starting the journey towards a second half career. I can assure you that pursuing a more fulfilling life won't necessarily fit into your perfect idea of sustaining life balance. Then again, what great person of note achieved their place in history by living a completely balanced life? Those who have accomplished great things have done so at immense personal cost, but it was worth it both for themselves and for others.

No regrets

When my kids were teenagers they liked to listen to Bon Jovi's song, "Live When I'm Alive, Sleep When I'm Dead." It was a big hit in the '90s. While I don't believe this song's message is entirely healthy, I agree with the philosophy of living life to the fullest. Just talk to any older person and you will quickly realise that the reward for taking risks can be worth it, but not taking risks may be something you regret forever.

One study that I found particularly enlightening on this matter of 'no regrets' is research gathered by a lady called Bronnie Ware, an Australian writer who once worked in palliative care. Her patients had been sent home to die, and she spent the last weeks of their lives with them. Through the course of many conversations she always tried to ask each patient if they had any regrets about their lives, and five common answers emerged:

EN**RICH**ED

1   I wish I'd had the courage to live a life true to myself, not the life others expected of me.

2   I wish I hadn't worked so hard.

3   I wish I'd had the courage to express my feelings.

4   I wish I had stayed in touch with my friends.

5   I wish that I had let myself be happier.

(*The Top Five Regrets of the Dying*, by Bronnie Ware. Balboa International Press, 2011)

If you're still worried about the risks involved in leaving your current life behind to enter a more enriched future, spend some time looking over those five regrets. If I had stayed in the game and not listened to that small voice inside of me, I'm convinced I would have expressed those same regrets as I sat in my rocking chair.

Thankfully, I closed my eyes, held my nose, and jumped. Now it's your turn.

" DON'T JUDGE EACH DAY BY THE HARVEST YOU REAP, BUT BY THE SEEDS YOU PLANT. **"**

– Robert Louis Stevenson

15 Making others successful

Many of us need a catalyst or a change of circumstance to get us moving towards living a more meaningful existence. It could be a death in the family, a health scare, an estranged relationship, or a wake-up call from someone we admire. Often, in times of adversity or strong emotional turmoil, we seem to gain the most clarity; this can then motivate us to change our priorities.

Regardless of the catalyst that got *you* to this point, hopefully by now you are keen and ready to play the best game you can for your second half and ensure you finish well. If you think it's too late or there's no way your life could be transformed into something resembling a noteworthy legacy – take courage from the true story of Alfred Nobel, the Swedish inventor who invented dynamite.

Alfred's two brothers Ludvig and Robert began their entrepreneurial careers by exploiting rich oilfields along the Caspian Sea and became extremely wealthy in their own right. As a result, Alfred Nobel also invested and amassed great wealth through the development of these new oil regions.

Then, in 1888 Alfred's brother, Ludvig, died while visiting Cannes. In a cruel twist of fate, the French newspaper that covered the story accidently published Alfred's obituary instead. In the short article, it highlighted Alfred Nobel's biggest contribution to mankind as his invention of dynamite. The obituary noted: "The Merchant of Death is dead" and went on to say, "Dr Alfred Nobel, who became rich by finding ways to kill more people faster than ever before, died yesterday." Alfred was greatly disturbed by what he read and was especially concerned with how he would be remembered. This event became the wake-up call that brought about his decision to create and leave a more humane legacy after his real death.

You see, Alfred Noble was a pacifist who never meant for his inventions to be used for evil. He invented dynamite as a safe explosive to be used for peaceful purposes such as road-building and mining. Unfortunately, world events at the time of his invention twisted his original intentions for dynamite and he was saddled with the moniker 'Merchant of Death' because it was used predominantly for war-faring.

On the twenty-seventh of November 1895, Nobel signed his last will and testament and set aside the bulk of his estate to establish the Nobel Prizes which today includes the Nobel Peace Prize, to be awarded annually without distinction of nationality. After taxes and bequests to individuals, Nobel's will gave the equivalent of US$250 million in 2008 to fund the prizes. The Nobel Peace Prize became the world's eminent award to reward someone who makes the biggest contribution each year in reducing armament and making the world a safer and better place.

The good thing that came out of the mistake the French daily made was that Alfred Nobel was able to rethink and realign his creative ingenuity and vast resources to leave a significant lasting legacy. He created something that would inspire and impact generations far into the future more than a century after his death.

In terms of wake-up calls, seeing your name wrongly printed in the obituary section of the newspaper is a pretty huge smack in the face, especially when your legacy is something that is untrue to who you are. Hopefully, you don't have to wait for a shocking circumstance to provoke you to take action. I know my own wake-up call wasn't quite so shocking but I'm glad I didn't wait for something bigger to happen before I re-assessed my priorities.

Let Alfred Nobel's story inspire you to try to create a legacy that you will be proud of and one that helps and changes other people's lives for the better.

Less is more

When we began this journey, I was standing in my beautiful home, wondering if the woman who had just pulled away from me would still be there in the years to come. My company, status and lifestyle had soared beyond my wildest ambitions; some might have said I was in an 'enviable position.'

These days instead of entertaining potential clients at elegant five-star restaurants, I'm content with a suburban coffee shop for lunch. By conventional standards, I've dropped a few rungs down the ladder of success as others climb higher and higher to positions of prestige and power. Those who once coveted my executive office would probably find this hard to comprehend.

You might think that's a bit hard to swallow for someone as competitive and driven as I am, but in reality I'm having the time of my life!

I'm working just as hard as before but instead of feeling as if my very soul is being drained by my work, I'm energised by it. Instead of dreading going into the office, I can't wait for the next day to start. And at the end of the day I truly look forward to going home, because Sue is still here. We have a great marriage and we have never been happier.

I used to think that the best thing I could give my wife and family was for me to achieve success so that the family would be well provided for – plus, a little dose of life's ample luxuries. But really, all they have ever wanted (all *your* family really wants) is the real you. A person who is happy and content with him or herself, and that seldom comes from us satisfying our own desires. Helen Keller, the first blind and deaf person in the United States to earn a college degree, wisely observed, *"Many persons have a wrong idea of what constitutes true happiness. It is not attained through self-gratification but through fidelity to a worthy purpose."*

She's right. And her notion was recently validated according to a research conducted by Dianne Vella-Broderick, Senior Lecturer in the School of Psychology, Psychiatry and Psychological Medicine at Monash University in Melbourne. The specialists in Dr Vella-Broderick's profession spend a lot of time trying to figure out what makes us tick, and in this particular study she was looking for what contributes most to an overall sense of well-being in humans. She surveyed 332 Australian adults, measuring the extent to which pleasure (self-gratification), engagement (immersed in activities that use our high-level skills) and meaning have in our lives. What she learned is fascinating and practically mirrors my own story.

According to her research, "pleasure did not play as significant a role in predicting subjective well-being as meaning and engagement." In fact, for some of her subjects, pleasure had a negative effect on them. In plain English, if you seek true happiness, find a way to use what you're really good at and invest in something bigger than yourself. Or as Winston Churchill once said, "We make a living by what we do, but we make a life by what we give."

Sowing new seeds

A few years ago one of our financial planning franchise-owners had pretty much hit the same wall that I had when I was still slugging it out in the trenches of the business world. A big, thickly-set, dark-haired guy, James lived in the rich and fertile Atherton Tablelands of North Queensland where he ran a successful financial planning business.

It was pretty clear to me that James was ready for a new challenge but he wasn't sure what it would be. He was restless, but didn't know why. The dream he had worked so hard to attain just wasn't delivering what he thought it would. He had paid off his house and put his kids through school, yet still there seemed to be loose ends in his life. He told me he wasn't sure if he should stay in business, sell it, or expand it. His lack of motivation and passion was uncharacteristic of this highly intelligent, driven and entrepreneurial businessman.

I invited him to join me and a group of business people on a trip to North India and he reluctantly agreed, on condition that he could fly business class all the way from Cairns to New Delhi. By the time he met up with us at our stopover in Singapore, he was already beginning to have second thoughts.

"I don't know why I agreed to this trip," he whispered to me in the waiting area. "As far as I'm concerned, India is a good place to fly over!"

I don't know if you've ever been to North India but it can be pretty daunting to first-timers, especially if you appear to be wealthy (which includes anyone wearing western clothes and walking as if they actually have some place to go). The second we got outside the airport in Delhi to catch a bus to our hotel, dozens of Indians besieged us, all trying to grab our bags, load them on the bus, and then get a tip. James didn't exactly appreciate the offer of assistance and responded somewhat undiplomatically.

"If you touch my bag I will kill you!" He roared.

I was beginning to wonder if James was cut out for being stretched like this and an incident a few days later did little to lift my pessimism. We were waiting to cross a chaotic Indian street to go to a restaurant. Everyone but James and I had made the mad dash through the traffic. He took one look at the bustling stream of cars, trucks, motorbikes, rickshaws, scooters and donkey carts and literally froze – the colour draining from his face.

"I have a wife and kids at home." He hissed. "I'm not crossing this road!"

We would probably still be there were it not for Shazu, our Indian guide, who gently but firmly led him across the road.

And then it happened.

We were walking along a street one night when he froze again, this time at the sight of families sleeping on traffic islands in the middle of busy intersections – men, women,little children, even infants.

"Don't they have homes?" He asked, clearly shaken.

The hope in their eyes

From that point on, he dropped his tough-guy façade and began observing his surroundings with a new set of eyes. He began talking less about himself and more about the social injustices around him. He was especially offended by the way Indian women were treated with less respect than animals.

But he also began to ask a lot of questions, and I could almost see his mind wrestling with ways to improve the lives of the people he had threatened to kill days before. We toured one of the children's homes where abandoned children are loved, fed, clothed, educated and protected from life on the street, and he was clearly touched by their smiles. Then we visited a sewing centre where women are taught how to sew and given a new sewing machine, thus having a marketable skill to earn their way into a better life. An entrepreneur himself, he watched with visible admiration as these women approached their new 'careers' with such vigour and earnestness.

When we next visited a church that Jossy had helped start, James' transformation was complete. It's not uncommon in India to ask a visitor to read from the Bible, and James was chosen on this particular Sunday. As he read from Psalm 23 ("The Lord is my shepherd, I shall not lack for anything") it all seemed to make real sense to him. These people had nothing, but possessed everything

– the knowledge that God loved them and that they were precious to him. Nothing else really mattered.

After he returned to his seat he leaned over and whispered to me, "It's in their eyes. These people have hope, they have hope in their eyes."

The irony is that for the first time on this trip with James, I saw the hope in his eyes. He had found the answer to that nagging feeling deep in his soul – purpose. Instead of pleasure, he opted for engagement and meaning.

A life transformed

On his return to Australia, James declared: "From now on, I want to use my business and use the money to invest in these people." Since that trip, James goes back twice a year to teach financial management principles to the community workers and church planters that *Empart* is training in North India. James has come to see what he is doing as a calling, and he is loving every minute of it.

Stephen Grellet, the Franco-American Quaker (1773-1885) once said, "I expect to pass through this world but once. Any good thing therefore that I can do, kindness that

I can show to any fellow-creature, let me do it now; let me not defer or neglect it, for I shall not pass this way again."

It is not just all about India. Opportunities to help others are limitless and know no borders. It's not about money. It doesn't cost much to volunteer once a week at a neighbourhood centre, teaching young people computer skills, for example.

It's about whether you want to make a living or have a life. It's about enriching your life by pouring as much of it as you can into others.

In one of his parables, Jesus warned against investing in things that don't matter – sounds like good advice to me, whatever your spiritual inclination:

Listen! A farmer decided to sow some grain. As he scattered it across the field, some of it fell on a path, and the birds came and picked it off the hard ground and ate it. Some fell on thin soil with underlying rock. It grew up quickly enough, but soon wilted beneath the hot sun and died because the roots had no nourishment in the shallow soil. Other seeds fell among thorns that shot up and crowded the young plants so that they produced no grain. But some of the seeds fell into good soil and yielded thirty times as much as he had planted – some of it even sixty or a hundred times as much! If you have ears, listen!

If the seeds of grain are your time, talent and treasure, where are you sowing them? If the majority of your time is spent growing your net worth, are you satisfied with the return you are getting from that investment? When you get home from the office each night, are you filled with a sense of accomplishment? Is your work adding meaning and purpose to your life? Can you honestly say that you are getting thirty, sixty, one hundred times the return on your investment of all that goodwill and energy?

If not, maybe it's time to look for some "good soil." Maybe it's time to share at least a portion of yourself with others and see what happens.

I have few regrets over spending the first half of my career building a successful business. If I had my time over again, I would have paid more attention to my family and maybe left the office early occasionally to enjoy life a little more. But, I truly believe that I was given a specific set of gifts and talents by God and that my first half was preparation for a second half of greater meaning and purpose. The satisfaction I now get from using those skills to make others successful far surpasses the pleasure I received from growing my business.

The challenge I faced, however, is one you may right now be facing – listening – being open to the stirring in your soul that I believe is the still, small voice of God inviting you to join Him on a great adventure. Too many people I know have missed it and appear to be on an endless and boring quest to find the next great holiday resort, the more exciting safari, the most remote beach.

If that sounds appealing to you, go for it. But, if you've stayed with me this far, you probably want so much more than that. So let me end our journey together with this challenge. Clear your calendar for a day. Go to that place where you are at your most creative, where you won't be interrupted and the ideas just seem to flow naturally. Take a note pad, your laptop, iPad – whatever you use to scheme and plan and record.

Then dream.

Imagine yourself free to be the person you really are. Jot down some ideas on how you can move from making a living to having a life. Don't try to solve all the world's problems or put together a detailed plan. Just brainstorm. Play "What if?" Give yourself permission to consider the jaw-dropping jump from where you are right now to where you really want to be. And don't be afraid to just close your eyes and listen.

At the end of the day, whether you are religious or not, recite this simple prayer: "My heart and hands are open; please show me the way."

My hope is that you will join a growing movement of idealists who believe they can change the world; men and women who know that the way to make their lives count for themselves is to make them count for others. Unconventional heroes who aren't satisfied with the good life; they want the best life – for themselves as well as the future generations.

After all, why settle for anything less?

" IMPOSSIBLE SITUATIONS CAN BECOME POSSIBLE MIRACLES. "

– Robert Schuller

Epilogue

Dear Reader,

Thank you for reading *Enriched* I hope it encourages you to begin your own journey of meaning and purpose. If you've already begun that exciting journey, then I hope you will be encouraged to think more intentionally about how you can inspire others to do the same.

Before you close the book, however, I'd like to share more intimately with you about some things that happened to me along the way that might have been difficult for you to believe until you finished the entire book and got to know me better. Some call them coincidences or good luck, but my story would be incomplete if I failed to share them with you.

As my life started to radically change its focus from myself to others, I noticed a trend developing – an illogical trend, in fact. So much of what has happened to me over the last twenty years just didn't make sense.

Take the financial windfall that I told you about earlier when the value of our company soared. The way the economy was at the time, it shouldn't have happened, but it did. The incredible thing was that something similar had happened a few years earlier when a major insurance company that owned forty-nine per cent of our company told us that they wanted to buy us out entirely. We went back to them and negotiated to instead buy *them* out. In the meantime, we found another company that agreed to buy forty-five per cent of our company, as we did not want to be left with a big debt on our balance sheet. They were willing to pay about fifty per cent more than what it had cost us to buy out the previous investor! And so, we made the first of our two 'too-good-to-be-true' deals. The profit I made from this first deal enabled me to wipe out my personal debt, relieving a huge amount of financial stress.

From a logical human perspective, these deals just didn't make sense. To be honest, it felt like someone was playing a giant game of chess and my business deals were the pieces.

Then there was the issue of my health, or lack thereof. My headaches were so severe that I could barely focus on my work. Only sheer determination and a little Dutch stubbornness kept me going. I tried just about everything to rid myself of the almost continual pain. I became fanatical about my diet, even becoming a vegetarian for about five years. I jogged and exercised regularly. I had blood tests taken, went to kidney and liver specialists, chiropractors, neurologists, naturopaths, and a few other specialists and alternative medicine practitioners. But nothing worked.

When I moved to Melbourne, so did my headaches. I kept trying to manage my health as best I could and continued to see experts in the hope of finding a cure, but to no avail. Then one day, as I was driving my car I was hit by the most excruciating sharp pain in my back–the worst pain I have ever known in my life. I was in complete agony. I didn't have a clue about what was happening to me, but knew I had to get to a hospital quickly. Barely able to drive, I headed for the nearest hospital but the pain got so bad that I had to pull over. 'Luckily,' I had stopped across the street from a medical clinic, so I made a beeline straight for it.

It turned out that I had kidney stones. Dr Shastra Naidu, general practitioner, was able to give me an injection that helped kill the pain. I talked to her about my headaches and asked if she could give me my usual strong painkiller prescription drug, but she refused. Instead, she ran some tests and discovered that I had fluctuating blood pressure.

So she began treating that and after trying some different medication, brought it under control. Not only that, but my headaches stopped! That was eight years ago and thankfully I have been headache-free ever since. I had been suffering from headaches since the age of fourteen.

What if I hadn't suffered a bout with kidney stones? What if I had been able to drive just that little bit further past that medical clinic?

As I focused more on helping others become successful, my relationship with my wife Sue began to improve. In fact, it started to grow and flourish, better than it had ever before. To put things in context here, whilst we had always been in love and had many common interests, we had begun to grow apart due to my neglect of her and the children because of my singular pursuit of my own success. I had become a workaholic. By default, this caused us to focus on our differences and pursue our own interests and as a result our relationship suffered.

Conventional wisdom would have said that we had grown too different and that our marriage just couldn't work, that those differences would always cause major problems, and that we should face the inevitable, get a divorce, and go our separate ways. Maybe, if we both had more compatible partners, we could have a real go at happiness.

If that's conventional wisdom, I'm so glad I ignored it! Sue is my soul mate and my best friend, and I love doing life together with her. But as you have read, it hasn't always been easy.

When I was focused on myself during the first half of my career, my domain was the business and her domain was the family. She wasn't really involved in the business and I wasn't really involved in the family, or at least not as much as I should have been. But, as I moved into my second half, I started caring more about Sue's success than my own – about the vision Sue had for *her* second half, and how we might make this exciting journey together.

And that's exactly what we are doing now. Before we were divided by our differences but somehow managed to cling on. Now, we are united by our vision and we love journeying together.

And what about that near fatal collision with the truck?

Certainly the driving conditions and my fatigue played a role in what could have been a tragic early ending to my life. But it also served to get my attention, leading me to ask the bigger questions about my life.

Coincidence?

That's one way of explaining these fortuitous events in my life. Another explanation comes from ancient wisdom that turns conventional wisdom on its head: if you want the best in life, put others first. To gain you must give. Money is not the true measure of your success.

I don't want to create the impression that following and practising the Christian faith guarantees that your marriage will work, your business will prosper and your health issues will go away. What I can say from my personal experience is this: once I aligned my life with the list of thirteen things I believe God had given me – once the primary focus of my life changed from myself to others – things changed for the better. The loneliness and frustration I had experienced before disappeared. I felt as if someone was walking beside me, and I found a new sense of peace that I had never known before.

Human logic would have said, "Don't embark on pursuing this new life mission until you get your health, finances and marriage all in order." But, I started doing it the other way around. If I had tried to fix all these things in my own way before I embarked on the amazing journey God had laid out for me, would I have found the cure for my headaches?

Would our business dealings have worked out or would we have gone bankrupt? Would Sue and I even be still married?

What about my kids?

Our four children are grown up now. They are all happily married and we have more grandchildren than I can keep up with!

Sometimes, I still regret the effects that my hectic, success-driven lifestyle had on our children when they were young, but thankfully, they all seem to have become very well-adjusted adults and parents.

Recently, I celebrated my 60th birthday in Melbourne with my wife, all of my children, and my amazing mother by my side. As we sailed off on a chartered yacht and enjoyed the scenic sights of the city I remember thanking God that things had turned out so well. Sadly, many of my friends and colleagues will never experience a moment like this as their relentless drive for success and accumulating more wealth cost them everything.

Knowing my insecurities about being a less than perfect father, each of my children had taken the time to write down some kind words. It was such a treat to hear their thoughts and memories, especially, when as a parent, we often only remember the things we wish we had done, or the things we did wrong and hardly anything that we might have done right.

So, let their words be an inspiration to you. Sometimes as parents we kick ourselves for every mistake, but at the end of the day, even if you did one thing right, that is something worth celebrating.

My eldest daughter Alice, who is now a devoted mother of three children, wrote the following, heart-warming letter:

"I admire that you have strong faith in God and are a man of great influence and integrity. I love it that you live your life to serve God and make a difference in the lives of the people you encounter.

I appreciate having a father who has a generous heart and lives to be a blessing to others. You have always been such a great provider for our family–and now that I am a parent, I realise how challenging that can be.

I am grateful that you always tried to be wise and responsible in your choices.

You have always worked hard for what you believed was right and I feel so blessed that you and mum have been happily married for nearly 40 years!! What a blessing to us children and the grandchildren and great grandchildren.

Thank you for this Christian heritage which you have faithfully shown by example to us over the years. With all my heart I am so thankful for this great legacy... such a treasure."

My son Heath, who now runs his own business and has three children wrote the following excerpt:

"I appreciate that you took me to soccer on cold, wet, Tassie Saturday mornings, even though you preferred Aussie-rules football. I'm glad that you inspired me to go further when we would go jogging early in the mornings. You taught me to compare myself to those who were doing well and not those that were doing badly.

You taught me to look at the big picture and to do everything from the perspective of long-term results.

I admire that you have shown and modelled that giving is better than receiving. Thank you for teaching me to focus on my strengths and not my weaknesses and to do the hard things even when they hurt.

You taught me to persevere and bounce back when things go wrong. You have never been precious about material things and you taught us not to hold tightly to possessions. You modelled that it is never too late to change, grow and develop. I am impressed that you never claim to 'know it all' and you are never dogmatic or legalistic.

I admire that you always worked hard to provide for your family and to give us the things that you never had.

I am grateful that my Dad has always had a heart for the lost, that you hold tradition lightly and that you care more about God's opinion than anyone else's.

I am proud that you have braved-up to the extent of even public speaking —now that takes guts. I'm impressed that you keep working, contributing to society and making the world a better place, even though you could have easily retired years ago and be living a life of leisure."

My third child, Renee, now a hard-working, loving mother of three, had these kind words to add:

"I appreciate that you let mum and I have horses and let us kids grow up with lots of pets (dogs, cats, horses, rabbits, budgies, cockatoos, etc.), even though you aren't an animal person and often incurred costly maintenance and vet bills as a result.

I am thankful that you moved us all back to Tasmania so that we could grow up in a safe and caring community. I am glad that we grew up in a close Christian environment with aunties, uncles, cousins and friends and that we felt part of a community.

You always worked hard to provide so well for your family and I am thankful that you passed your strong work ethic down to us.

It's always been comforting to know that we can come to you for advice but you always let us make our own decisions and give us all our own space to grow.

Even though you were busy and had such terrible headaches, you took the time to take us on family holidays where we were able to create lifetime memories.

As an adult, it's so precious that we always have a loving home to come to with our own children when we visit you in Melbourne."

And my youngest daughter, Jessica, now a business owner and a mother, ended with these words:

"I admire that you worked so hard to provide for your family. You made huge sacrifices for us to have a great childhood in a safe, Christian community in Tasmania, and it was such a great foundation for us kids.

I am grateful that despite working long hours and suffering crippling migraines we went on holidays and were able to take our friends with us; that's a lot of kids in a small space. I don't know anyone whose parents did that. I am impressed that you always seem to have ten balls in the air – and are always helping an organisation or someone in need. I am really proud of your generosity towards people.

I am grateful that for better or worse, it is your voice in my head which speaks reason, attacks problems logically, and looks at the bigger picture.

I am so thankful that we were always well fed, well looked after and went to good schools. I never questioned your love for us, even though you were busy.

You and mum provided such a solid Christian model of life for us kids. We always went to church, read the Bible and prayed as a family. Now that I'm a parent, I realise and cherish what great habits you instilled in us. I hope I can pass on this legacy."

Whilst these letters did not contain all the mistakes I had made as a parent, they highlighted the things that I did right and for that, I was truly grateful. I hope that by sharing my children's words and memories, you are inspired to imagine your future to be bigger and better than you have ever dreamed.

It might be too late to change all the mistakes you have made in the past, but it's not too late to change the future.

Up until my defining moment, I saw my work as separate from my spiritual life. I believe the evidence above challenges that view. The late Henry J. M. Nouwen, an internationally renowned Catholic Priest and prolific author once wrote, "We seldom realise fully that we are sent to fulfil God-given tasks. We act as if we were simply dropped down in creation and have to decide to entertain ourselves until we die. But we were sent into the world by God, just as Jesus was. Once we start living our lives with that conviction, we will soon know what we were sent to do."

My defining moment showed me what I was sent here to do: help others succeed and experience and share the true meaning of enrichment. And I believe if you pay attention to the quiet voice in your heart, you too will discover the God-given task that will transform your life and turn it into an adventure.

Today, more than ever, people are reading self-help books and exploring various forms of spirituality. I have read and benefitted from many of these books, but since I rearranged my priorities the book that has inspired me the greatest is the most popular book every printed: the Bible. Meditating on it daily has revolutionised my life. If you have never read it – or tried to but couldn't get past the "thee's" and "thou's," get a copy of "The Message" version by Eugene H. Peterson. Go to your favourite bookstore or buy on line at www.amazon.com. It's written in today's language and articulated in the most wonderful conversational style.

Today, I work with many successful leaders to help them find their Ephesians 2:10 calling which is about how all of us are "created for good works that God prepared in advance for us to do before we were born." I feel so privileged to get a ringside seat to observe massive positive changes happen as people discover they are here for a greater purpose than they could ever dream of.

I would like to encourage you to embark on a journey that promises to be the most thrilling adventure of your life. It's a journey that is both practical and spiritual.

My prayer for you is that you will discover how much you will gain from giving. Coming to terms with making others successful literally gave me my life back, and it will do the same for you!

John Sikkema
July 2012

Acknowledgments

This book was many years in the making, mostly because I gave up on it several times. In fact, I might have never finished it had I not applied an important business principle to this project – you need a great team.

To get the project over the line, I was blessed to have found a group of talented individuals with specialist complementary skills – people who brought passion to the common vision of producing a book. I am forever grateful to these outstanding individuals who made time in their busy schedules to give priority and their talents to this project.

Any business success I have achieved came from having just the right people coming alongside me at just the right time, and the same is true of this book. I am indebted to many good people who shared their skills and knowledge, encouraged me when I didn't think I could finish it, or read it in its various stages and provided helpful suggestions for making it better.

The main credit for this book goes to Lyn Cryderman, a "top notch" editor and writer from the US who helped me develop the storyline and then organised the content into that structure.

Much credit must go to Andy Drewitt who patiently used his journalistic skills to extract many of the stories and important background information, to Owen Salter for his wisdom and guidance and David Cheah whose ongoing encouragement kept moving this project along to it's eventual completion, for which I am extremely grateful.

A big thank you goes to Tim O'Neill for his clear thinking and excellent memory which added valuable and vital missing content at a critical point in the project; Keston Muijs for his amazing skill in the brand development area and commitment to delivering a very high quality look and feel to the book; John Muys for his valuable publishing advice, and Lesley Williams at Major Street for her assistance in publishing the book.

I could not have finished this book without the invaluable assistance of our daughter Jessica Whitehill. Her creativity and critiquing skills played a crucial role in getting me to finish the project and ensured the stories I conveniently left out were included! The support and contribution of each of our children, Alice, Heath, Renee, and Jessica, have been very much appreciated.

A special word of appreciation goes to my close friend, Jossy Chacko, whose continual encouragement, advice and wisdom helped convince me that I should write this book and kept me going when I wanted to quit.

Greg Murtha, who works for the American organisation, Halftime (www.halftime.org), has to be the most positive can-do guy on the planet, and it was his motivation that helped me make the final push to finish this book. Thanks Greg! Thanks also to the entire team at Halftime for their encouragement and constructive feedback, especially CEO Dean Niewolny, Lloyd Reeb and Jeff Spadafora.

The 'Halftime movement' was started by Bob Buford, an American entrepreneur. I am a beneficiary of Bob's unique leadership, wisdom, generosity and ongoing encouragement, and I am indebted to him for writing the Foreword.

My appreciation also goes to the many different people who read different manuscripts and gave invaluable feedback that helped me come to the point where I was confident in the final product.

The final but definitely not least key member of this team, of course, is my wife Sue. I simply couldn't have written it without her unconditional love, wisdom and practical support. Thank you, Sue!

I also want to acknowledge and thank my parents (my dad, the late Jan Sikkema and mum Tina Sikkema) for their love, Christian heritage, faith and values that they modelled and handed down to me. These are the most precious things a parent can give a child. I am especially thankful for my mum, whose sharp mind, despite her advancing years, was able to describe in detail numerous stories of which I had only vague recollection.

Ultimately, this book is a testimony to an amazing God and Heavenly Father who, despite my stumbling from time to time, has guided my life and blessed me way beyond what I deserved.

References and Bibliography

Bronte, Lydia *The Longevity Factor* (Perennial, 1994).

Buford, Bob Halftime: Moving from Success
to Significance (Zondervan, 2008).

Chacko, Jossy *Madness* (*Empart* 2008)

Collins, Jim *Good to Great* (Harper Business 2001)

Covey, Stephen *7 Habits of Highly Effective
People* (Free Press, Revised ed 2004)

Deutschman, Alan *Change or Die: Three Keys to Change
at Work and in Life* (HarperBusiness, 2009)

Friedlander, Judy. *Career Moves in Philanthropy*

Gerber, Michael *E Myth* (HarperCollins 1995)

Hybels, Bill *Holy Discontent* (Zondervan 2007)

Luks, Allan *The Healing Power of Doing Good* (iUniverse, 2001).

Peterson, Eugene H. *The Message Bible* (Message 2005)

Piesse, Emily "Business Links Help Students,"
WA Business News, March 1, 2007.

Robinson, Ken *The Element: How Finding Your
Passion Changes Everything,* (Penguin, 2007)

Semler, Ricardo *Maverick* (Grand Central Publishing 1995)

Stanley, Andy *Visioneering* (Multnomah Books 2005)

Upkins JR, Louis *Treat Me like a Customer* (Zondervan 2009)

Vella-Brodrick, D. A., Park, N. A., & and Peterson, C. (2008). "Three ways to be happy: Pleasure, engagement and meaning – findings from Australian and US samples." Social Indicators Research, 90, 165-179

Ware, Bonnie *The Top Five Dying Regrets of the Dying: A Life Transformed by the Dearly Departing* (Balboa Press, 2011)

Warren, Rick *The Purpose Driven Life* (Zondervan, 2002)

Useful Websites

http://www.*empart*.org

http://www.halftime.org

http://www.actionforhappiness.org

http://michaelhyatt.com/find-your-passion-in-three-steps.html

http://www.drphil.com/articles/article/73

"No correlation between wealth and happiness: Study," *The Times of India,* March 20, 2009 (online version: http://articles.timesofindia.indiatimes.com/2009-03-20/ science/28025946_1_happiness-legatum-institute-prosperity.

Friedlander, Judy *Career Moves in Philanthropy,"* (http://www.3pillarsnetwork.com.au/ knowledge/behaviour_change/social_impact/ career_moves_in_philanthropy/k42)

http://australianetwork.com/nexus/stories/s2102590.htm

Contact us

Thank you for taking the time to read *Enriched*.

If this book has inspired you or if you can identify with its key messages, we would like to hear from you.

Please log onto www.enriched.com and send us your feedback online. Or email me directly at john.sikkema@enriched.com

We will send you a **complimentary and comprehensive 30-60-90 day plan** to kick start your own personal journey to live an enriched life full of impact and adventure!